Zurab Tsereteli

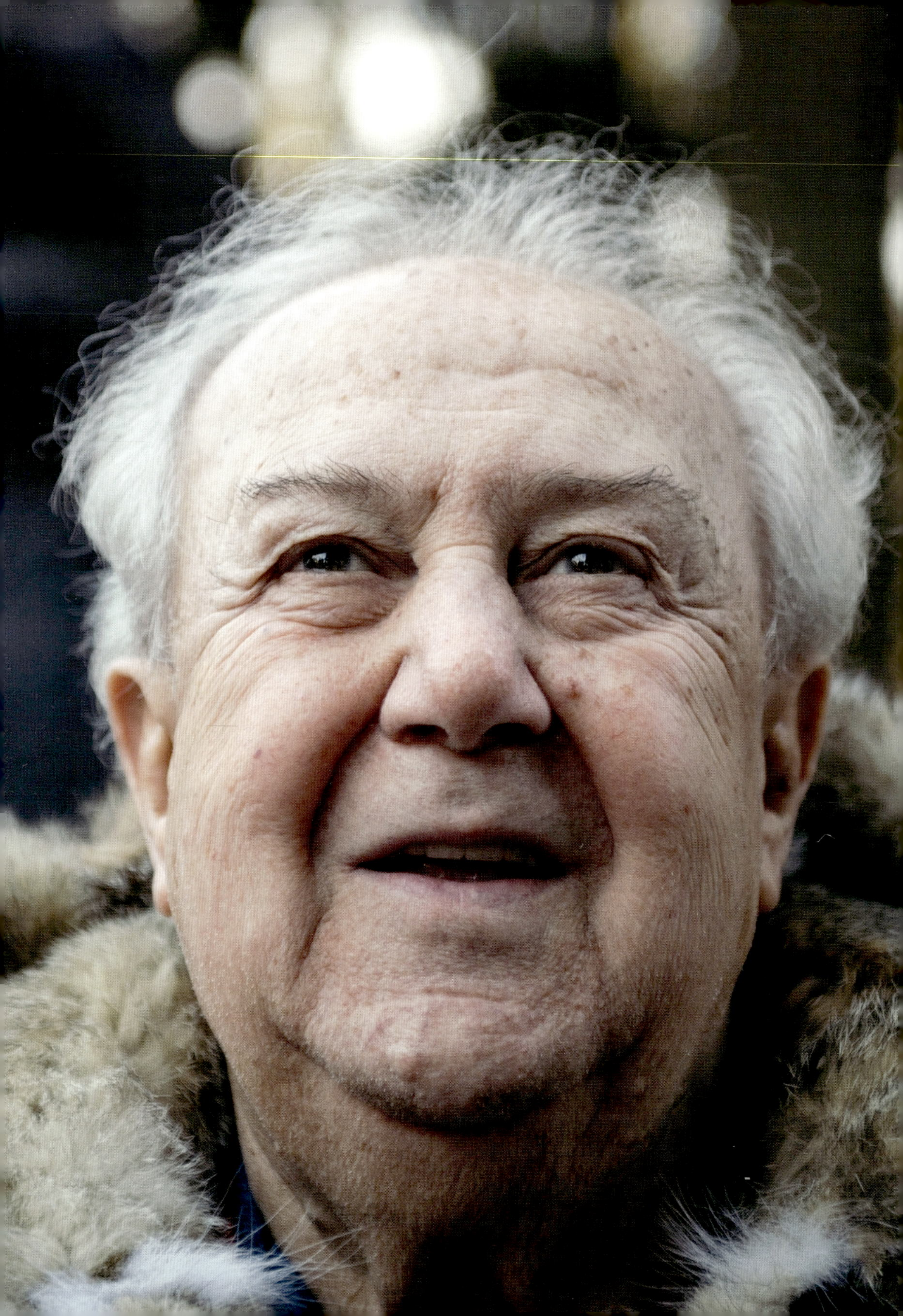

Zurab Tsereteli

Photographs by
James Hill

SKIRA

Editor
Paola Gribaudo

Art Director
Marcello Francone

Design
Luigi Fiore

Editorial Coordination
Vincenza Russo

Editing
Emily Ligniti

Layout
Fayçal Zaouali

First published in Italy in 2019 by
Skira Editore S.p.A.
Palazzo Casati Stampa
via Torino 61
20123 Milano
Italy
www.skira.net

Printed and bound in Italy.
First edition

ISBN: 978-88-572-4040-4

Distributed in USA, Canada, Central & South America by ARTBOOK | D.A.P. 75, Broad Street Suite 630, New York, NY 10004, USA.
Distributed elsewhere in the world by Thames and Hudson Ltd., 181A High Holborn, London WC1V 7QX, United Kingdom.

Contents

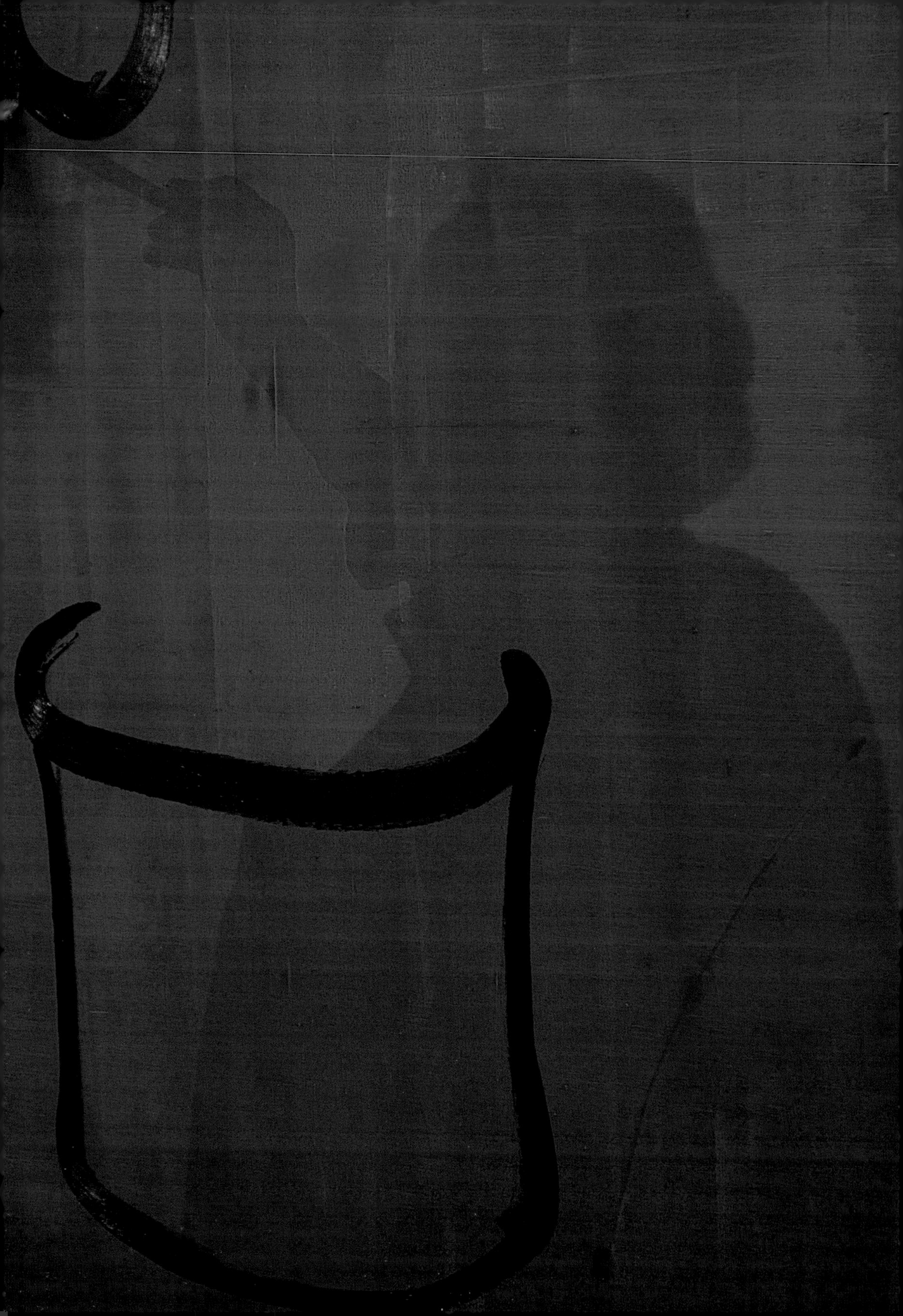

Zurab Tsereteli

James Hill

A few years ago, Vasili Tsereteli, the director of the Moscow Museum of Modern Art, approached me with the idea of spending some time with his grandfather, the artist Zurab Tsereteli.

I had never met Zurab Tsereteli, but after living for many years in Moscow there was probably no one whose work was more familiar to me. I had driven or walked countless times past his statues, but what Vasili was curious to capture was something far more intimate: his grandfather's painting.

So I went to visit Zurab Konstantinovich, as he is known to his friends, in his three studios in Moscow as well as those in Paris and New York.

In every location, I found something different. At Prechistenka in Moscow, which is also home to the Museum and Exhibition complex of the Russian Academy of Arts, the studio felt like a communal space. During the course of the day, Tsereteli would sometimes be alone, but more often he was surrounded by school children or artists or by friends who simply came to say hello. The space felt to me like a cross between a studio and a living room which, I came to realize, is also because Tsereteli does not try to separate his work from his daily life, since for him they are intrinsically interwoven.

This is surely part of his Georgian heritage and his extraordinarily sociable nature. Nothing gives him greater pleasure than to gather everyone after a day of painting for a late lunch, presenting a table invariably so laden with dishes that the tablecloth is invisible to the guests.

His studio near the Trocadero in Paris, however, is very different. Here the rooms and corridors are narrowed by paintings unable to find room on the wall. It is a much more intimate and private space though, even in Paris, there were constant interruptions as Tsereteli's friends dropped by for a chat or a cup of tea, even if he would barely pause from painting. It was usually only late at night that Tsereteli found himself alone, accompanied by the rotating beams of light from the Eiffel Tower, just across the river.

New York, too, where the studio is located on the top floor of a house just to the east of Central Park, is calm and pensive. During the January days when I visited, cool, steely light would flood the room at one moment and then be replaced by a soft, cloud-diffused gray. The atmosphere would change, and Tsereteli would pause for a moment to adjust a color slightly. Each time he started a new canvas he would look for a friend to paint or an object in the studio—perhaps flowers or a porcelain animal would catch his eye. There was never any question of taking a break. Even in his eighties there is a necessity, not only a desire, to pick up his brushes and paint.

Back in Moscow he also spends time at his studio on Bolshaya Gruzinskaya, which is the largest of his studios, framed by towering walls and artist busts. On the weekends he heads to Peredelkino, just to the south of the city. The village of Peredelkino has, since Soviet times, been a refuge for the capital's artists and writers. Pasternak and Voznesensky made their homes there and Tsereteli's house and studio stand at the end of a road surrounded by tall pines. Everything is quiet and restful except for Tsereteli himself who, immediately after breakfast, walks straight to the studio.

Moscow, 2018

The Studios

Prechistenka
Moscow

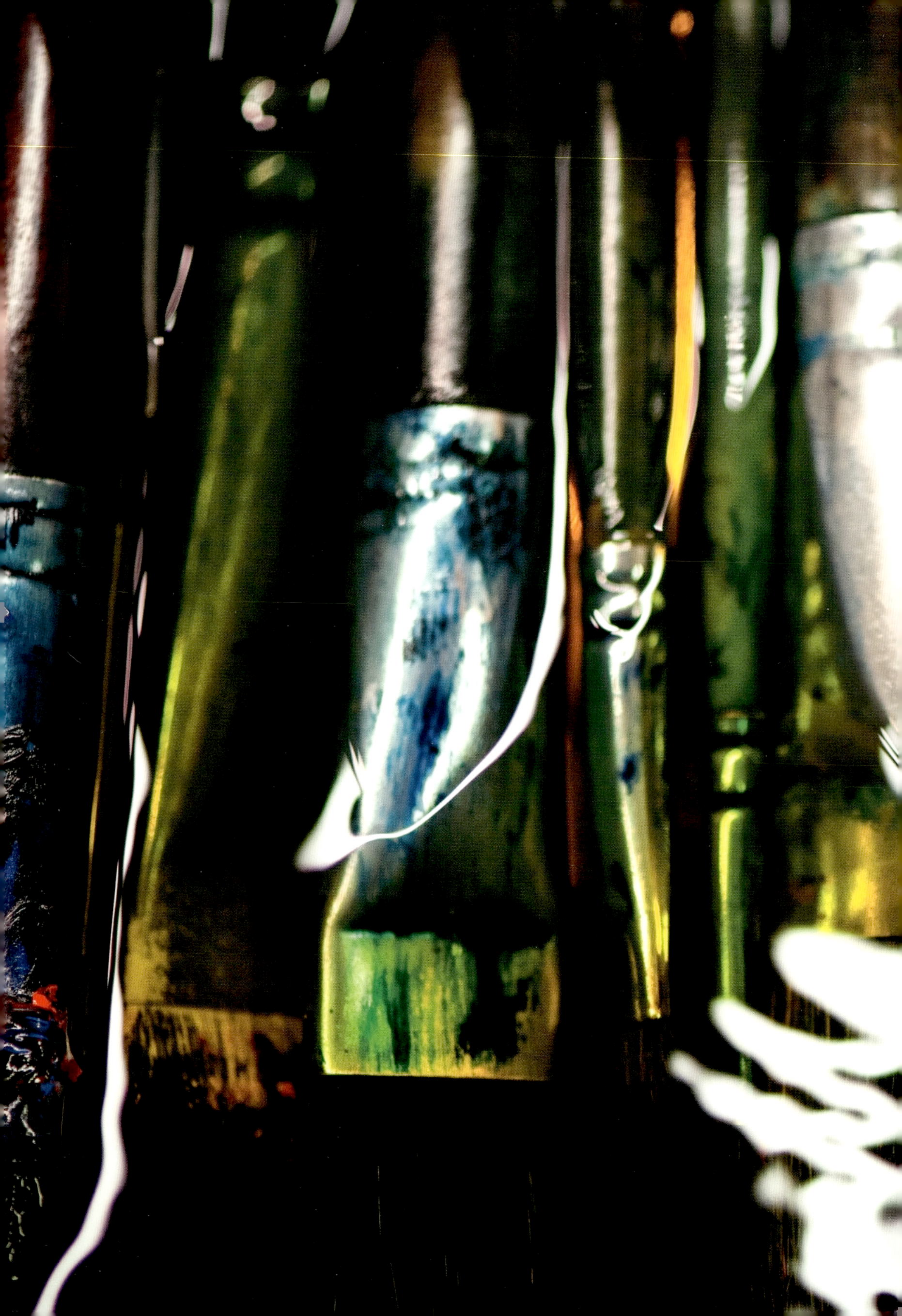

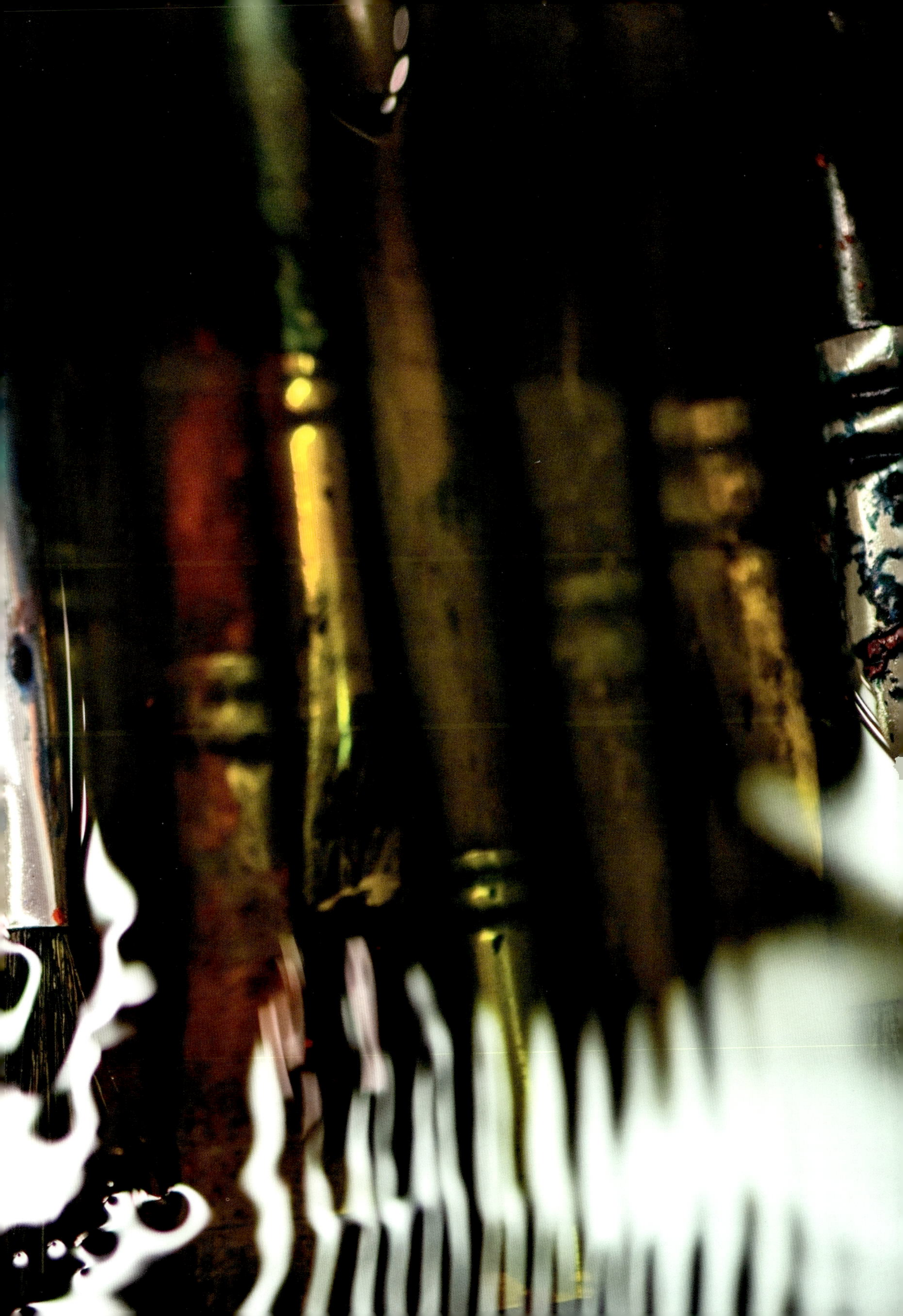

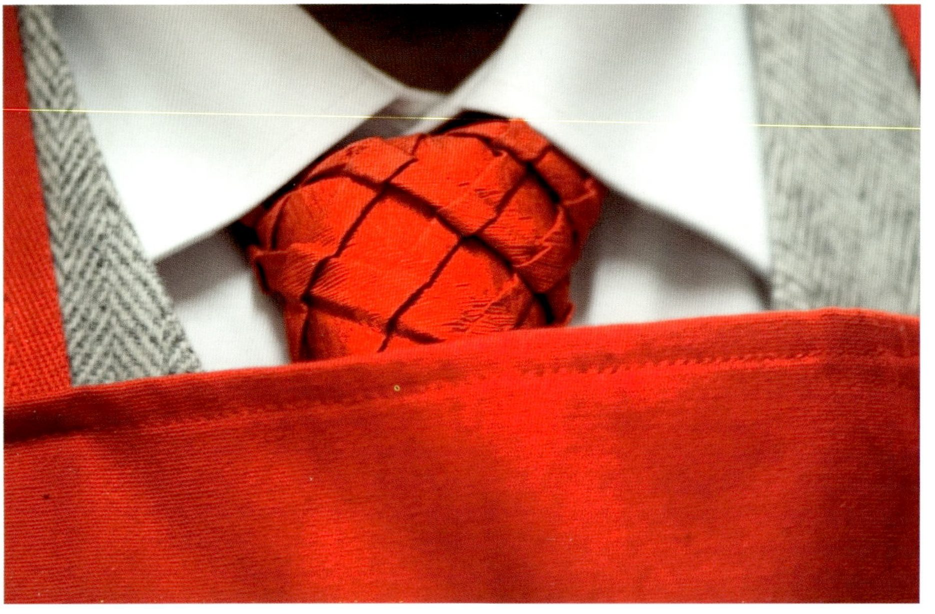

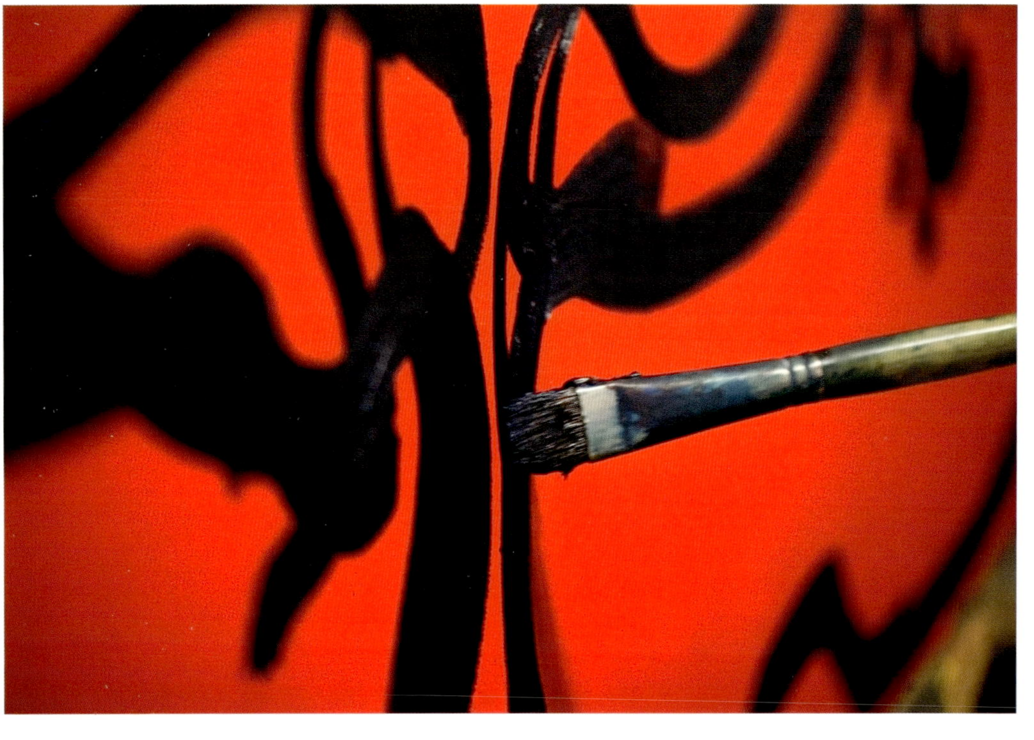

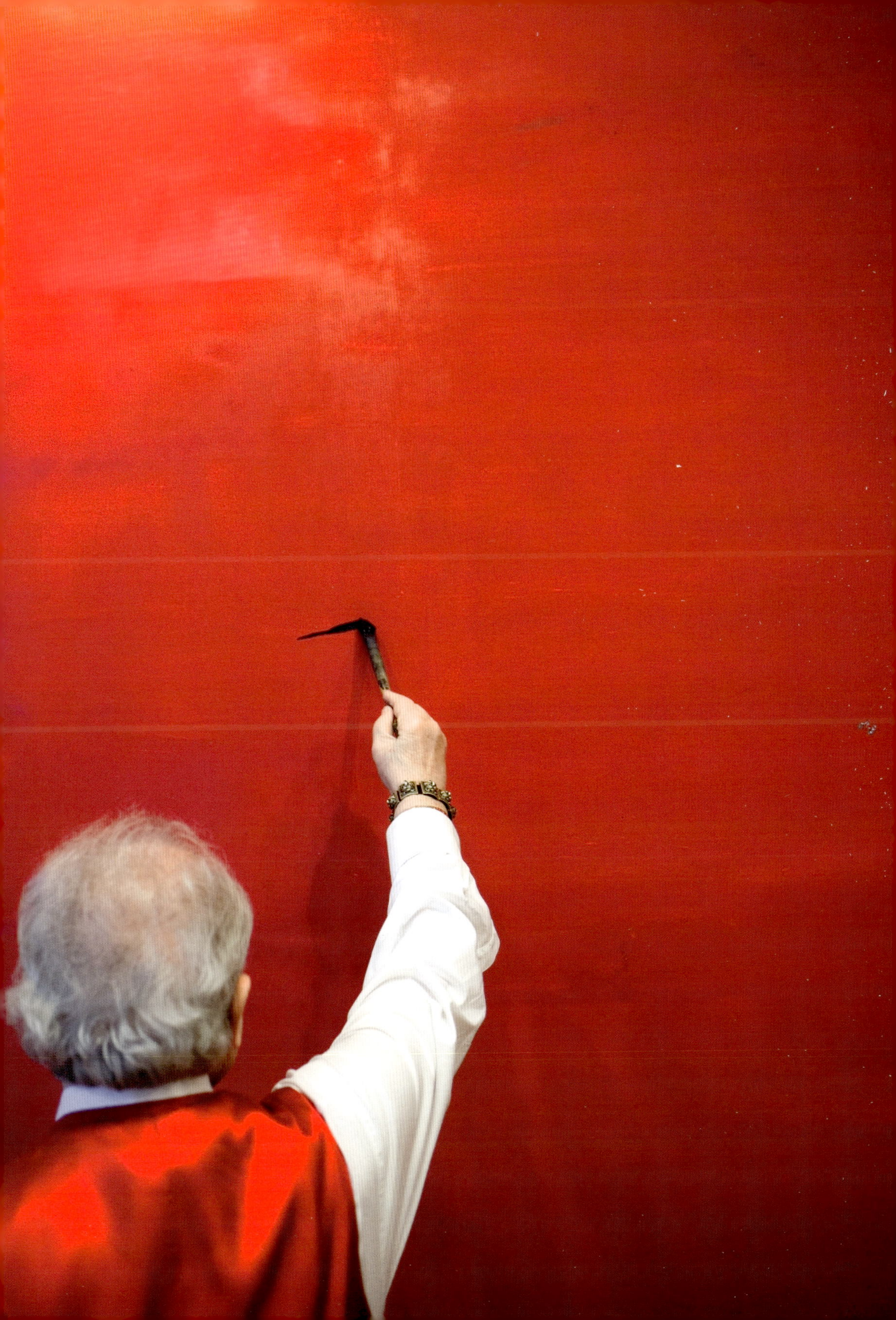

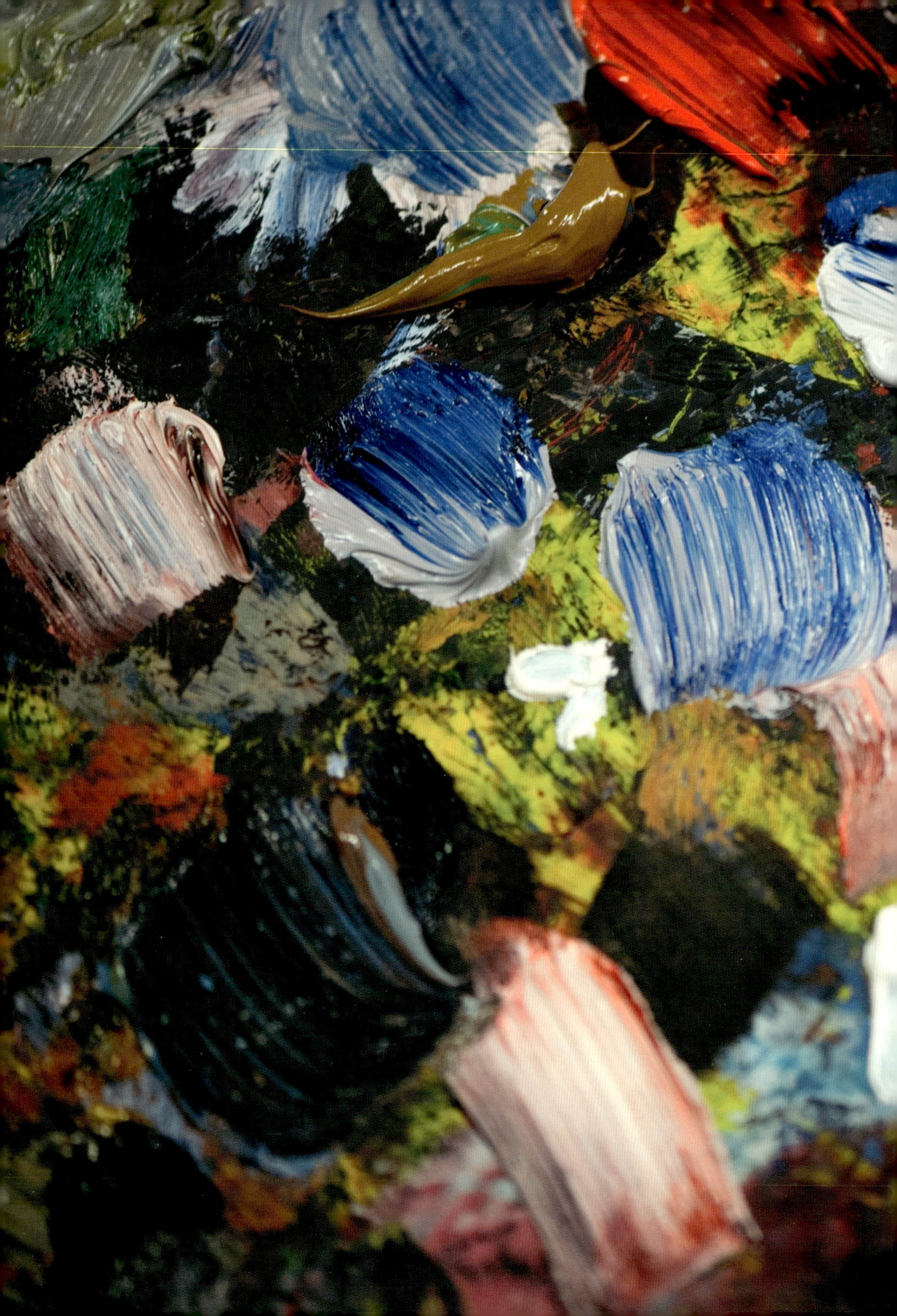

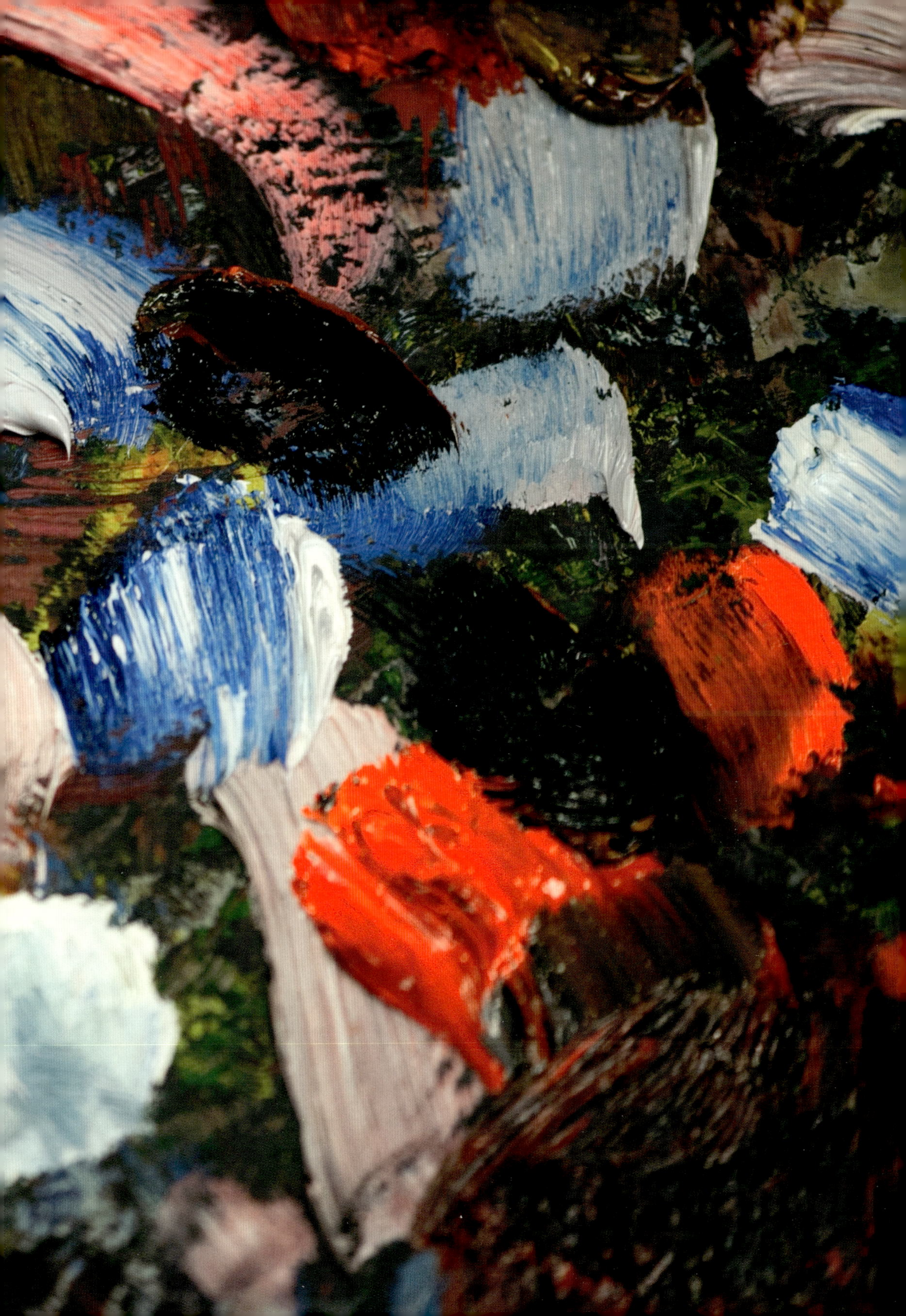

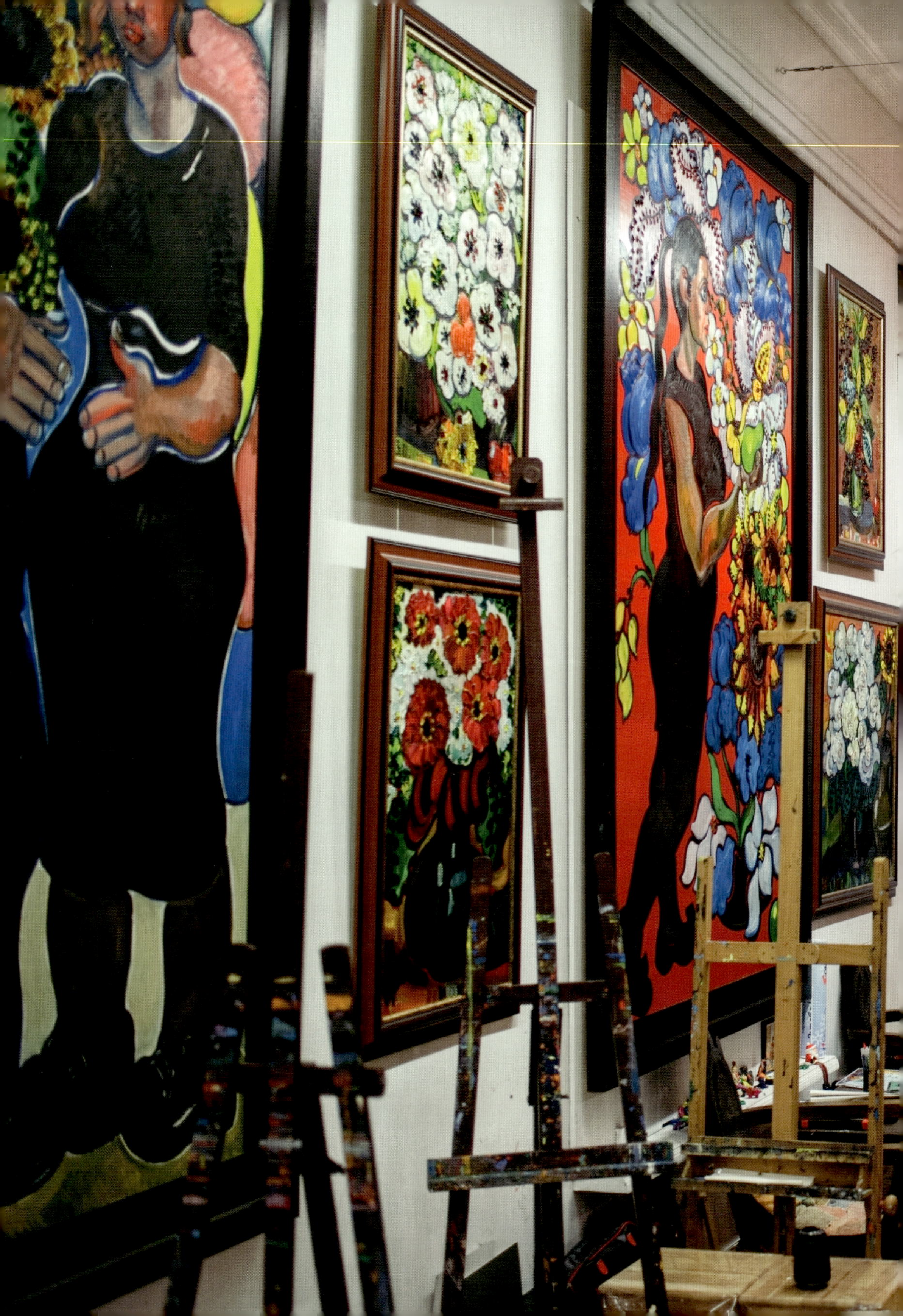

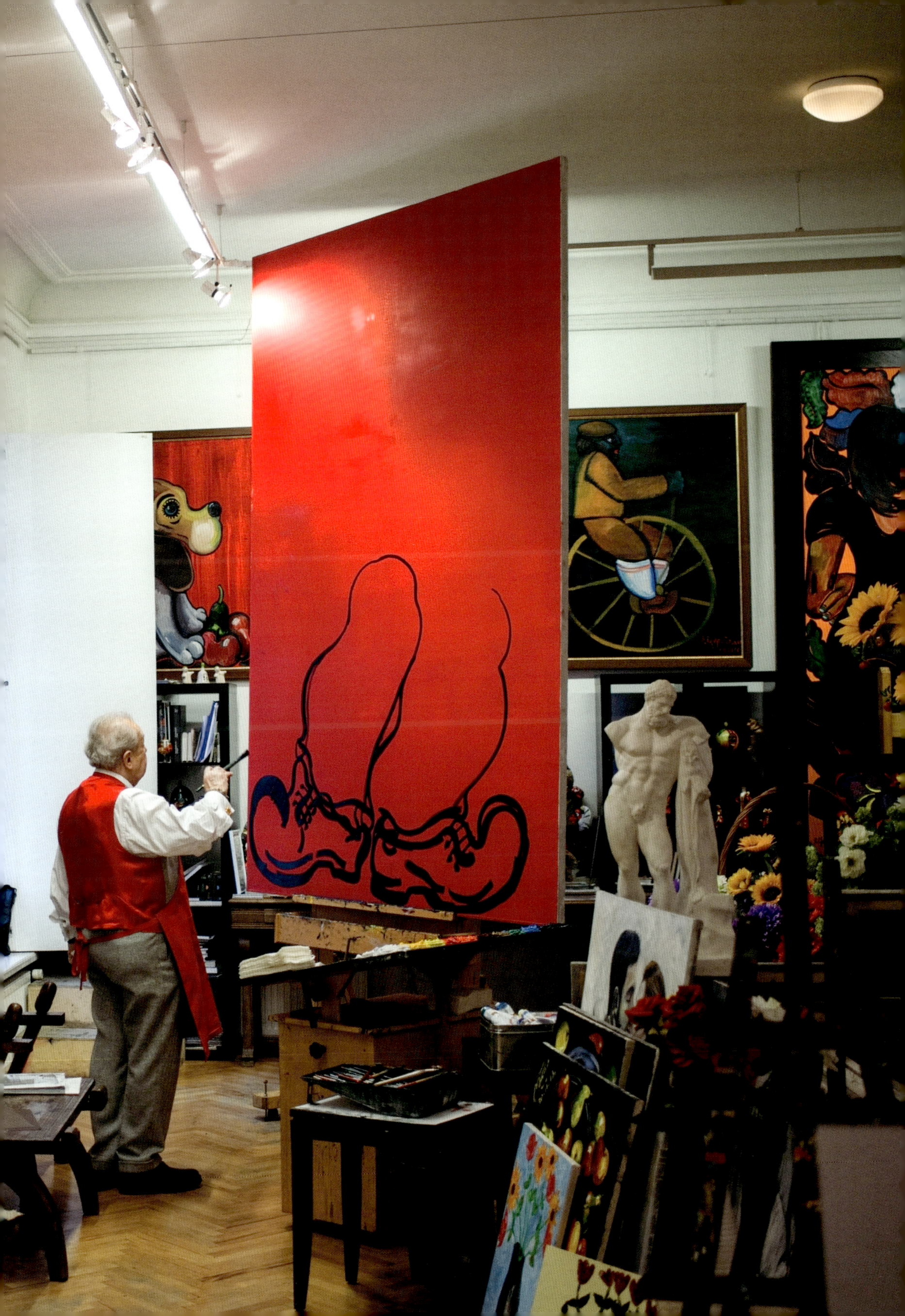

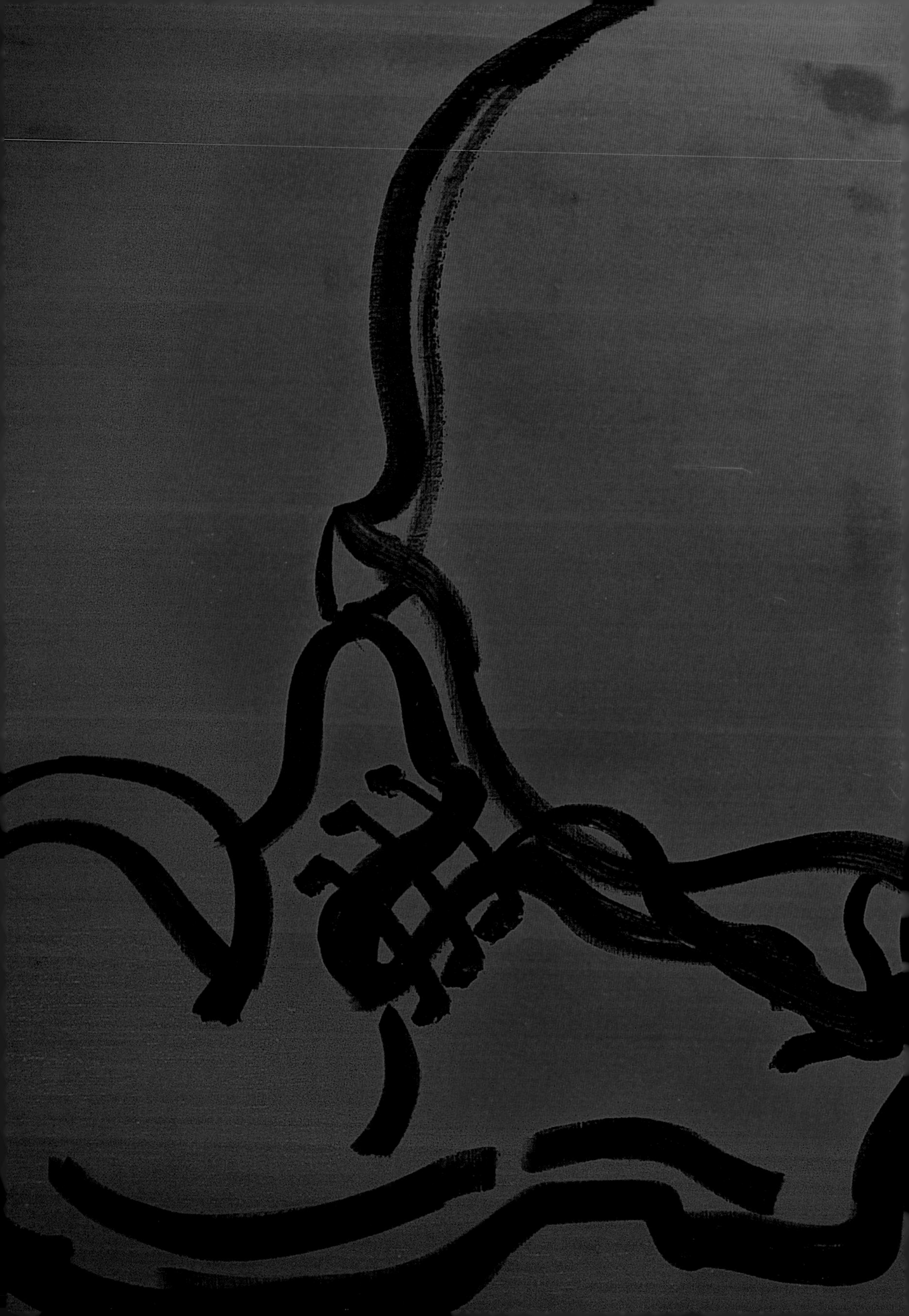

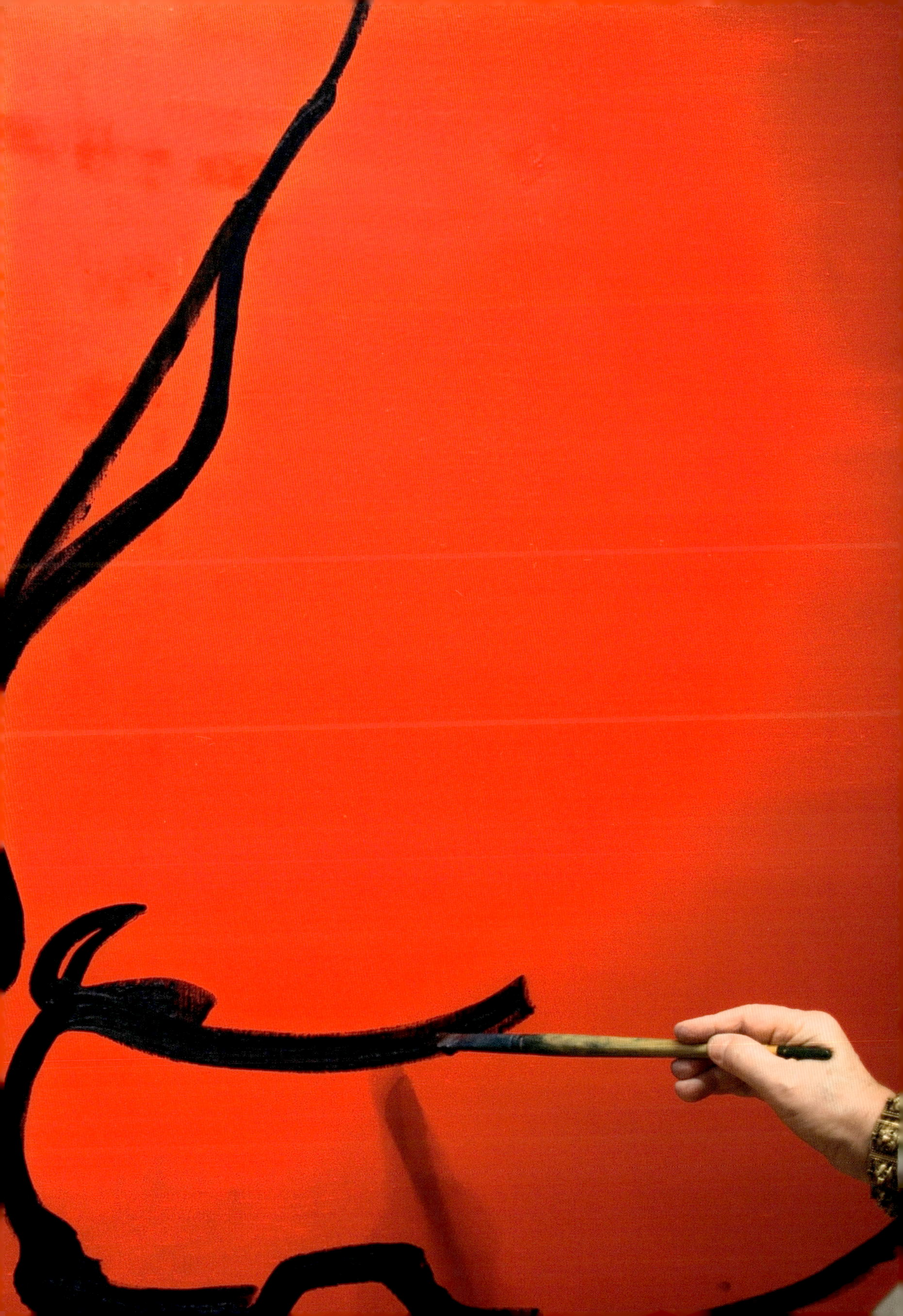

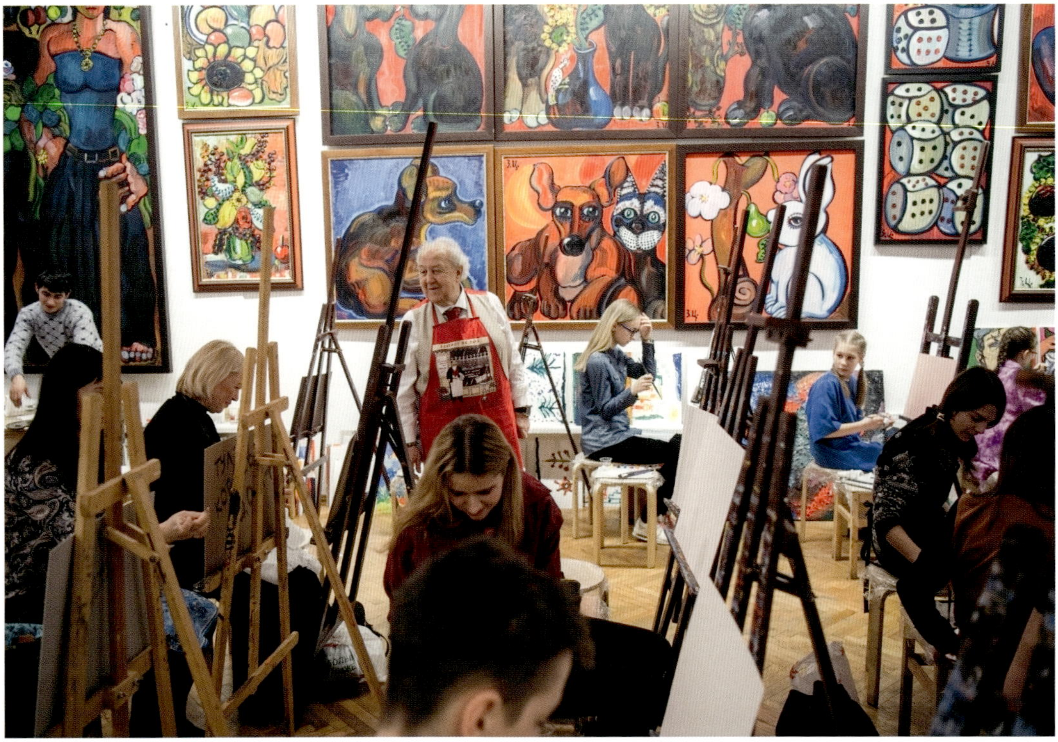

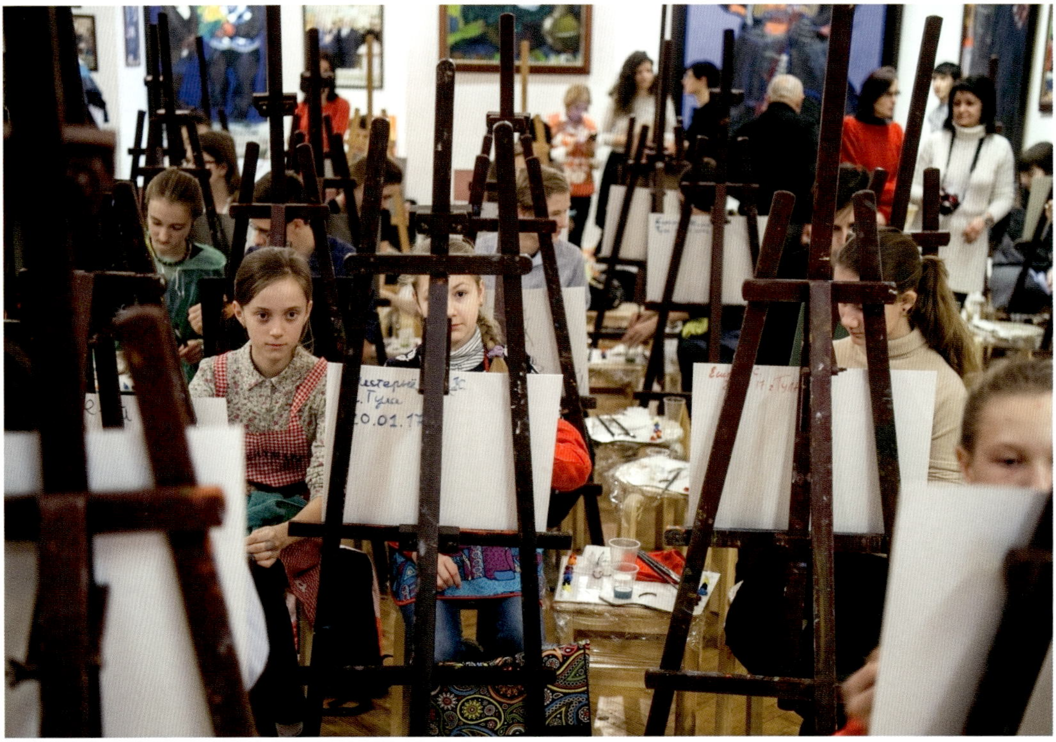

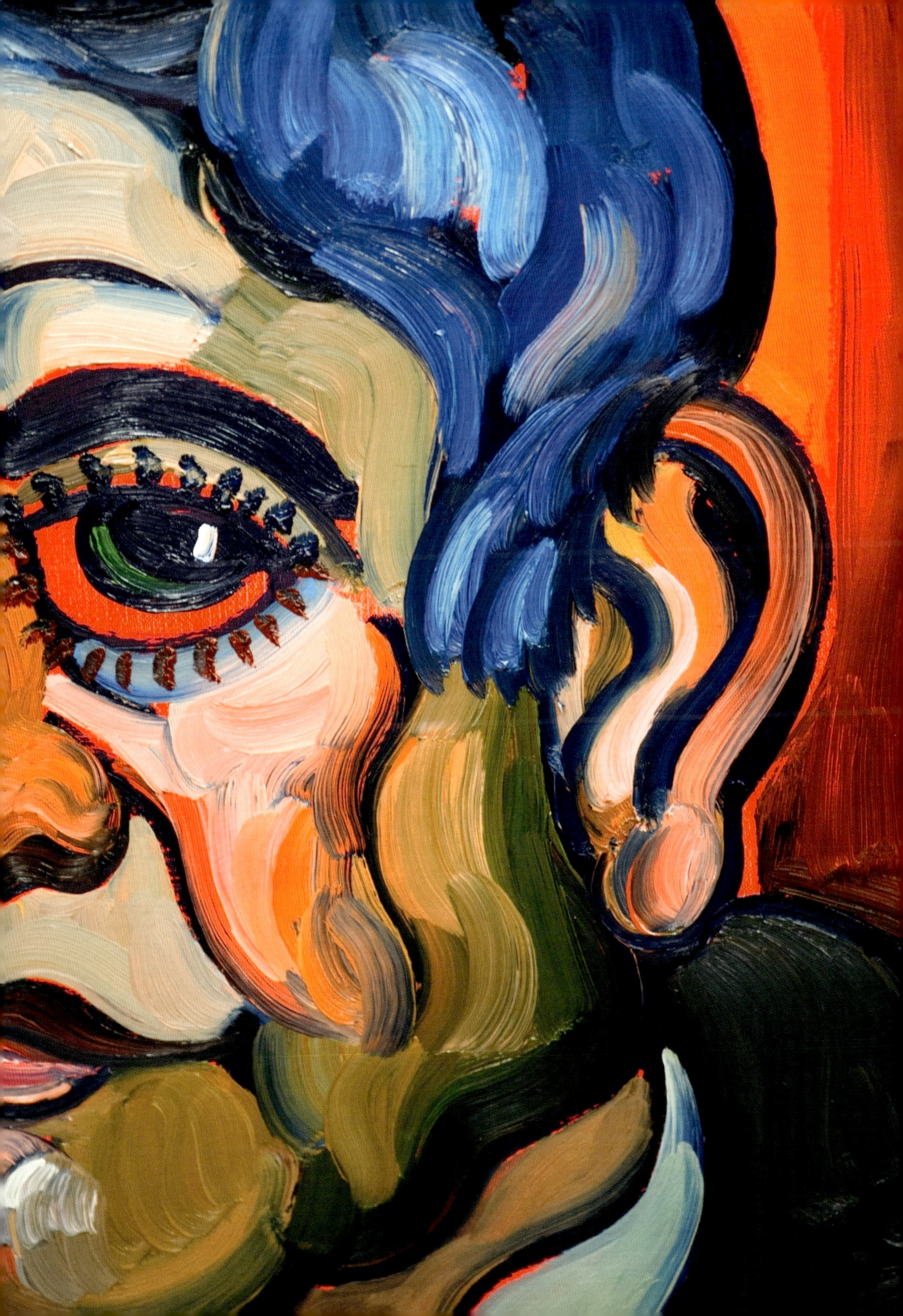

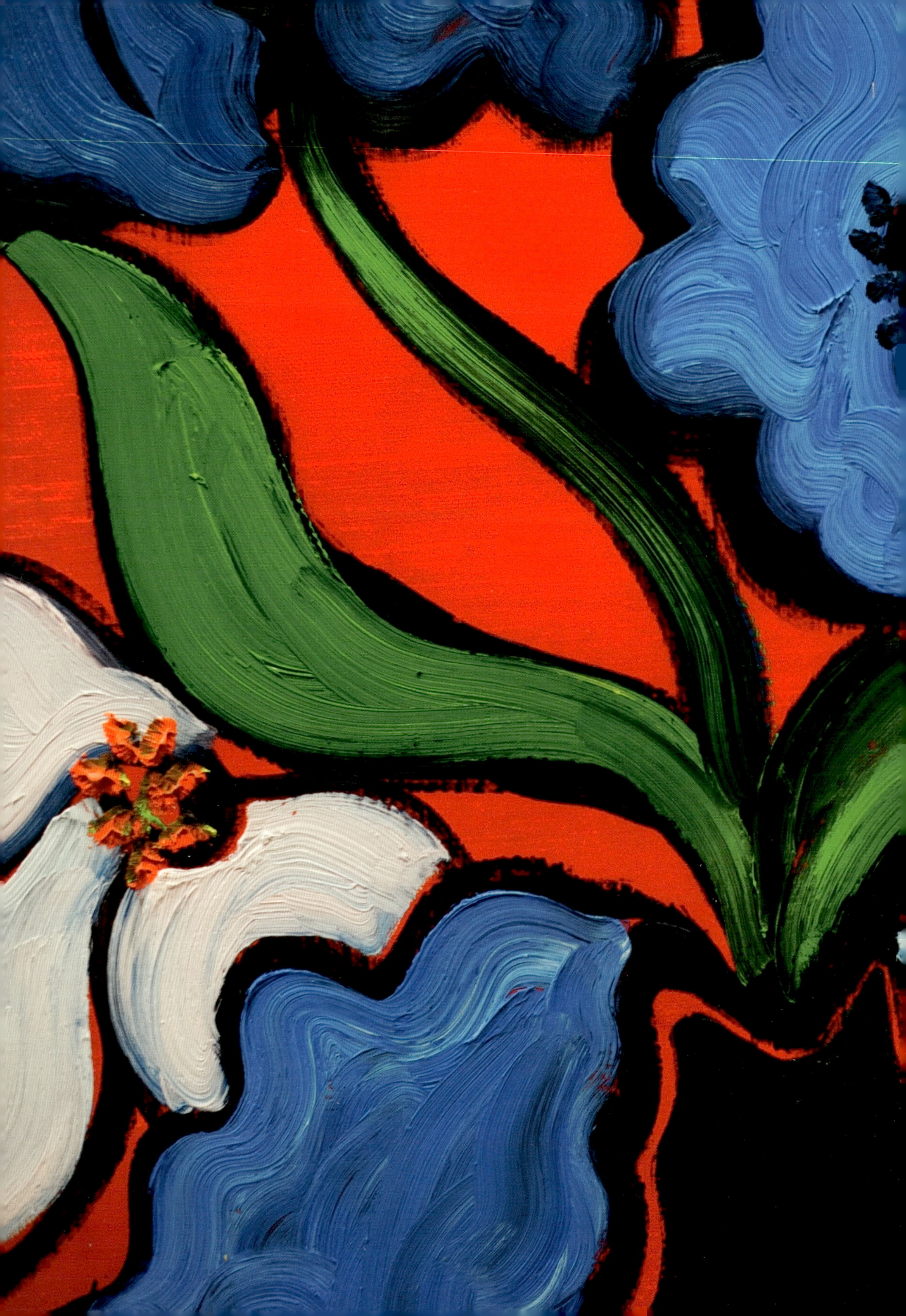

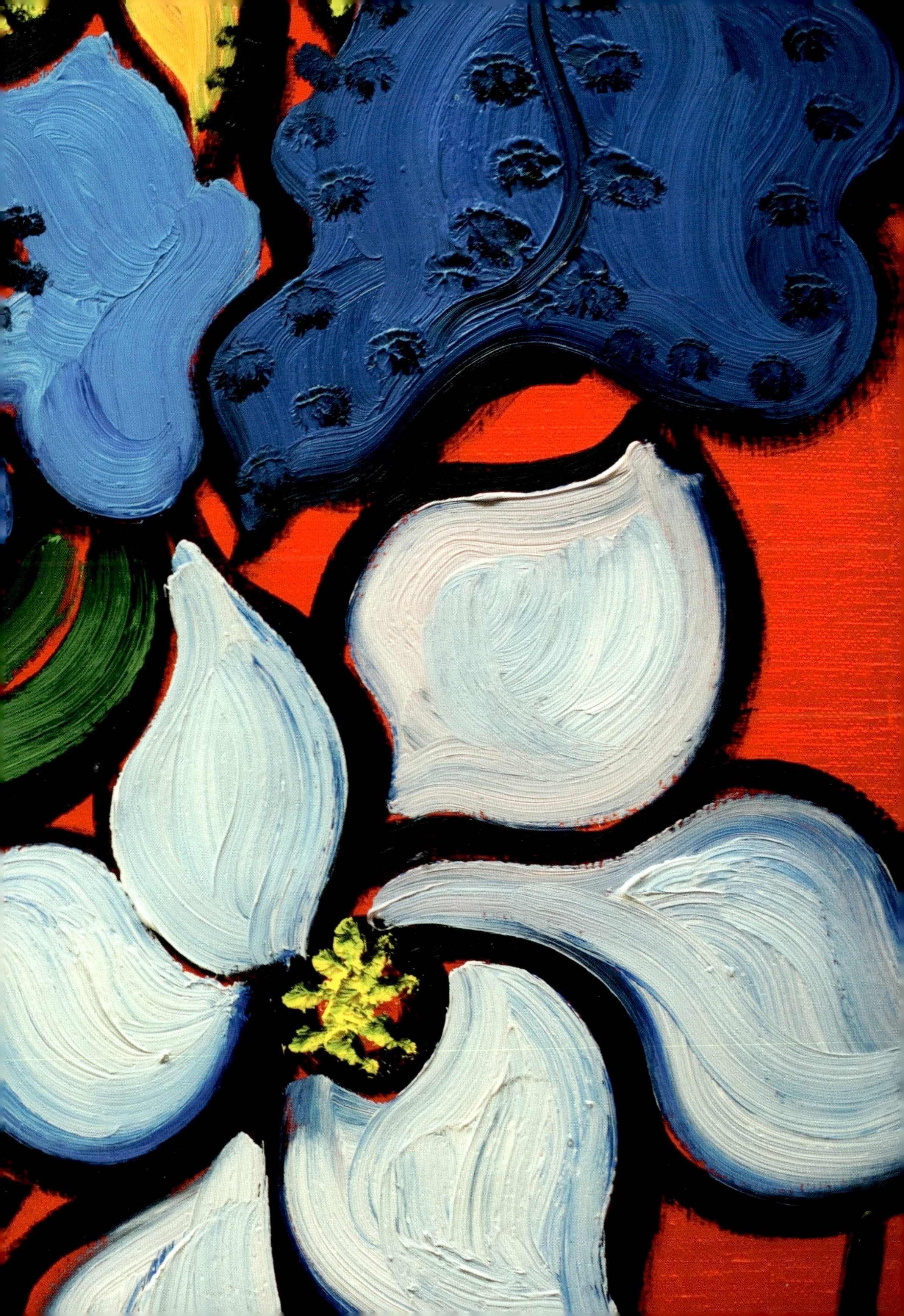

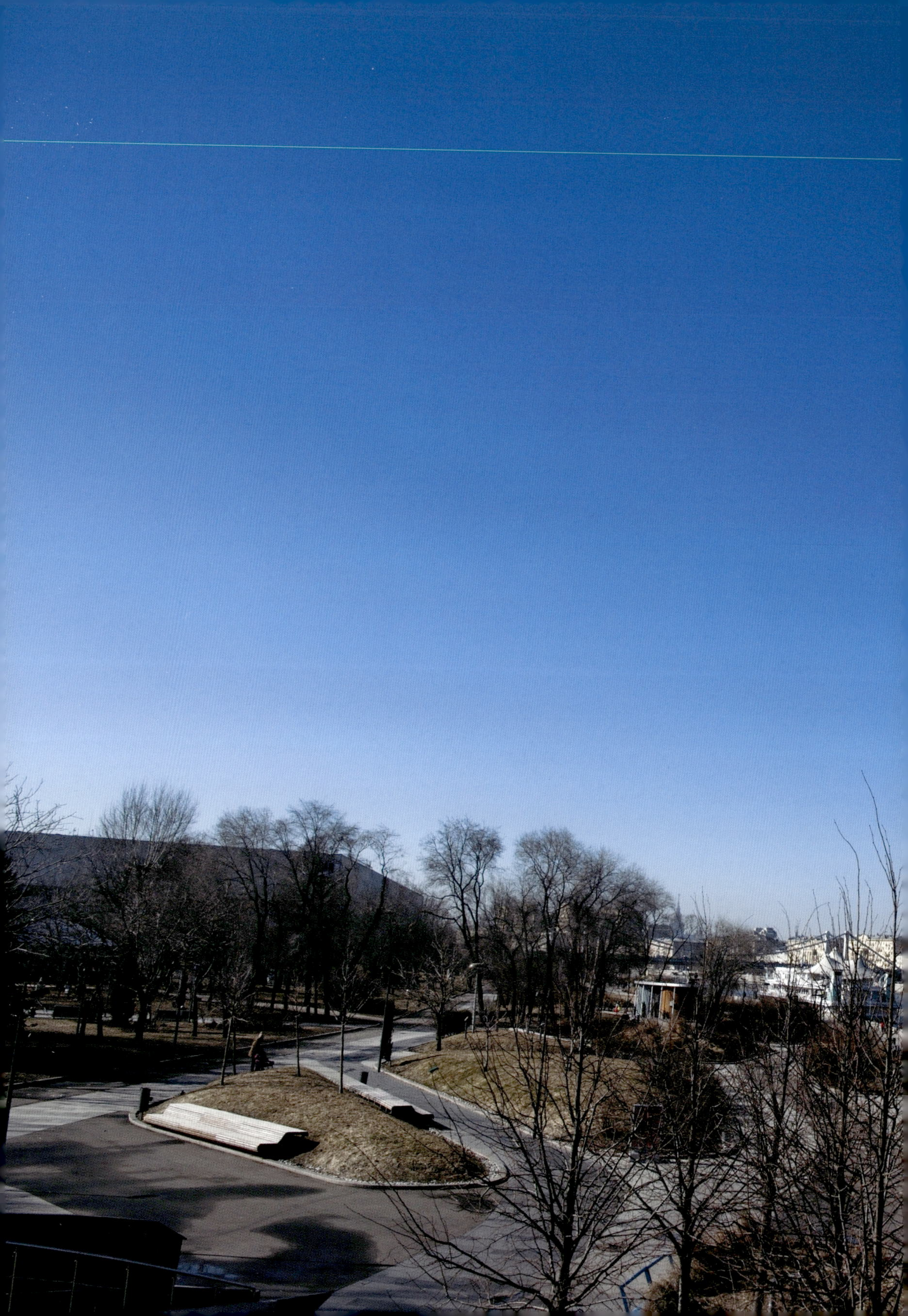

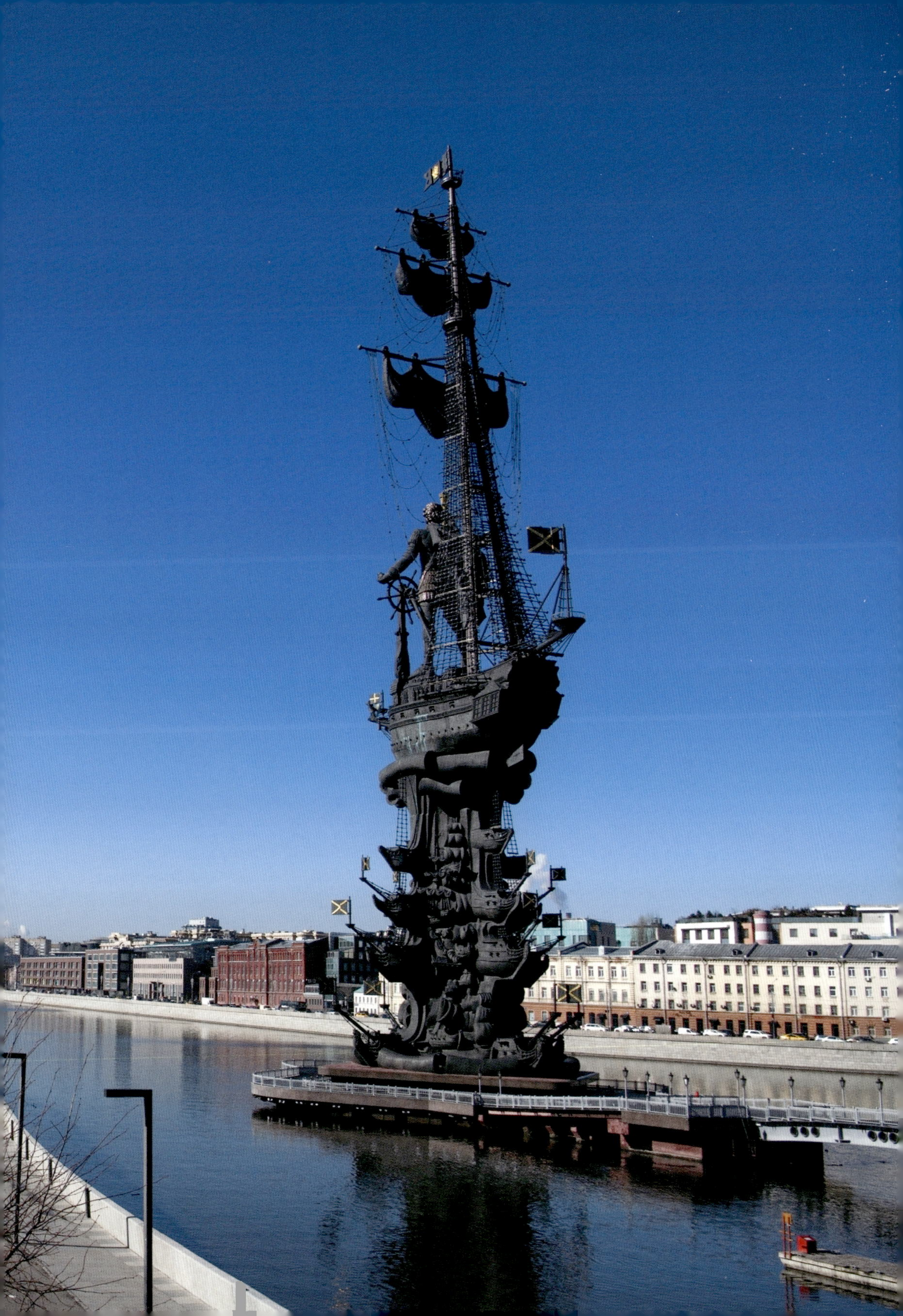

Bolshaya Gruzinskaya
Moscow

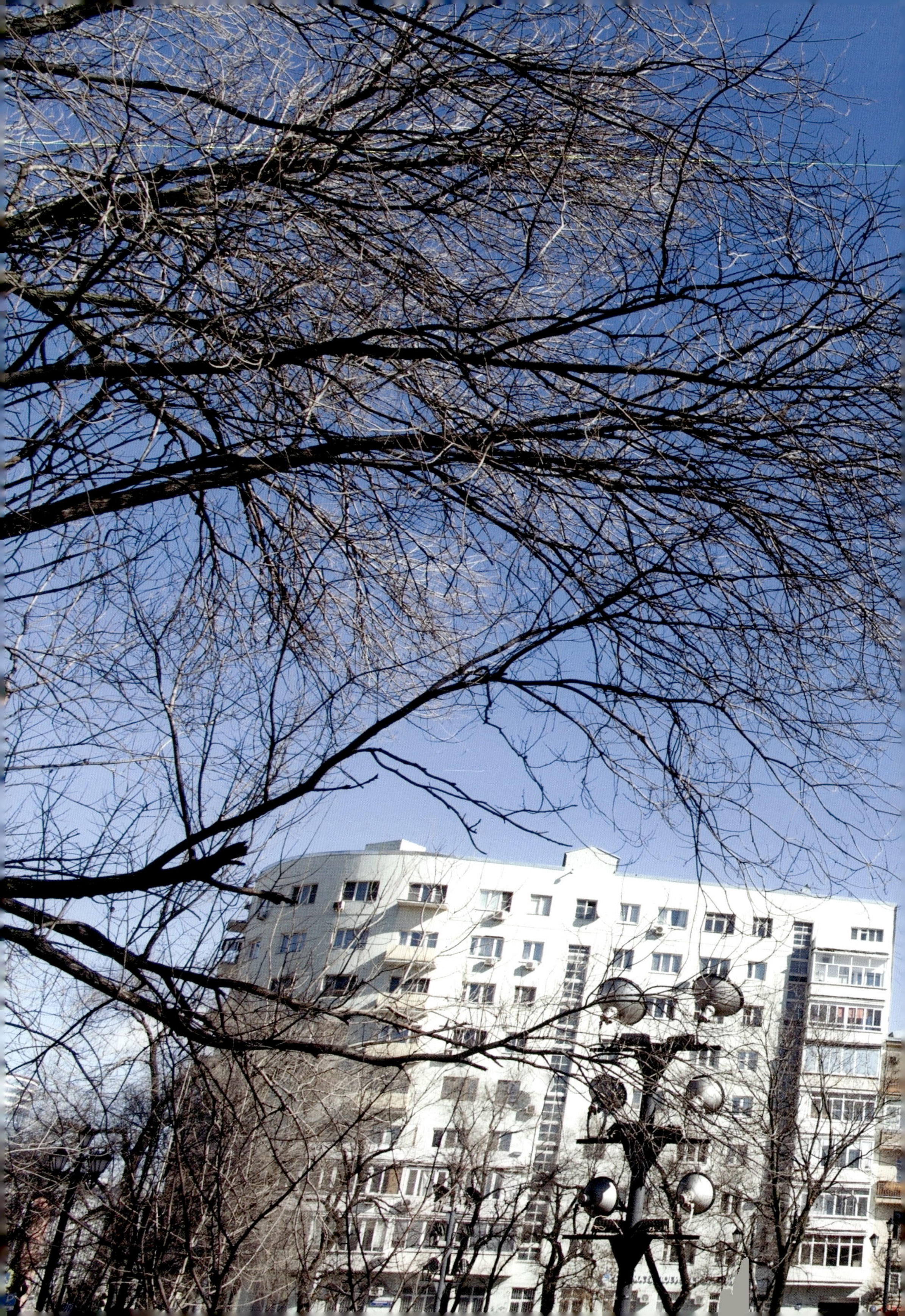

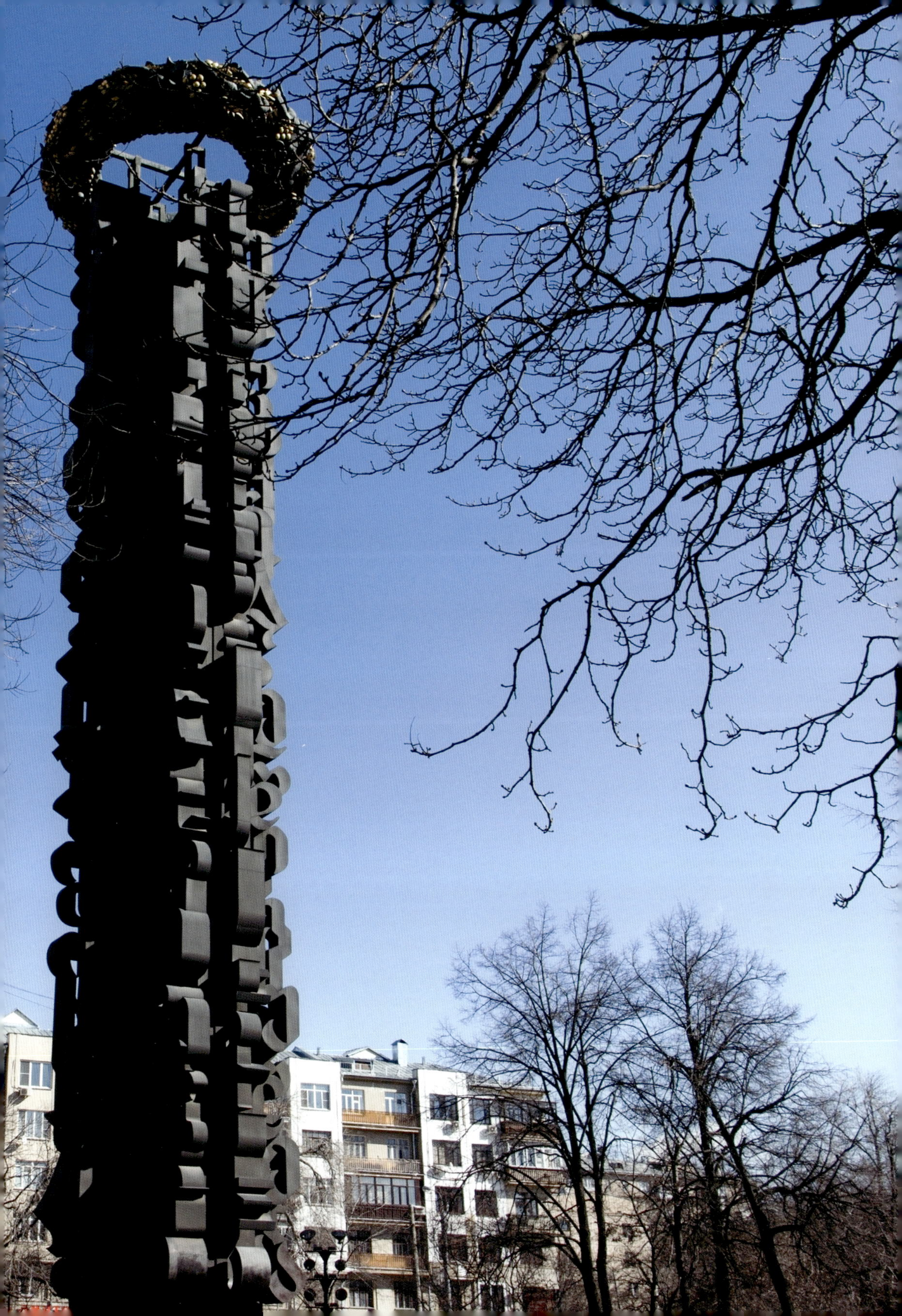

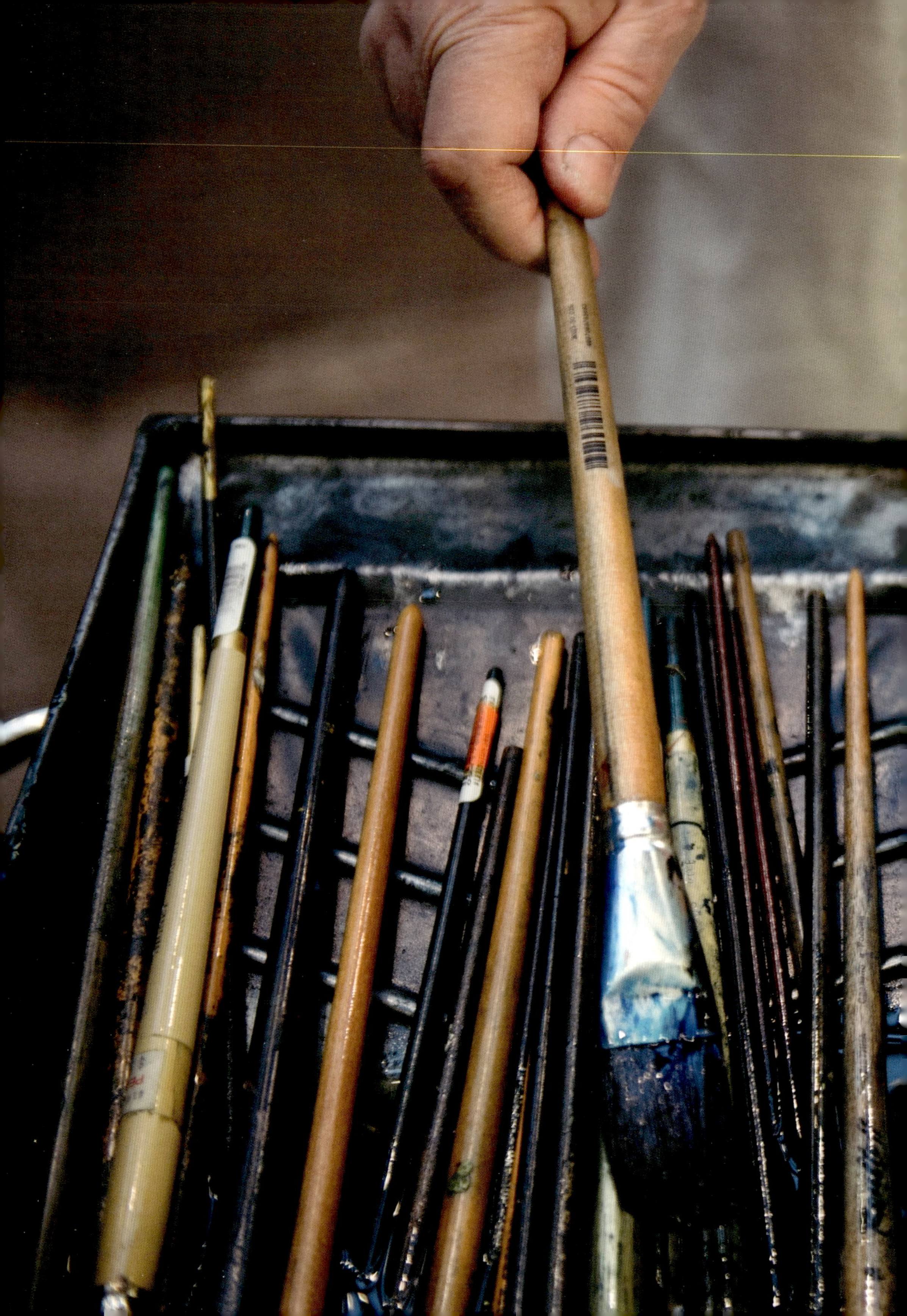

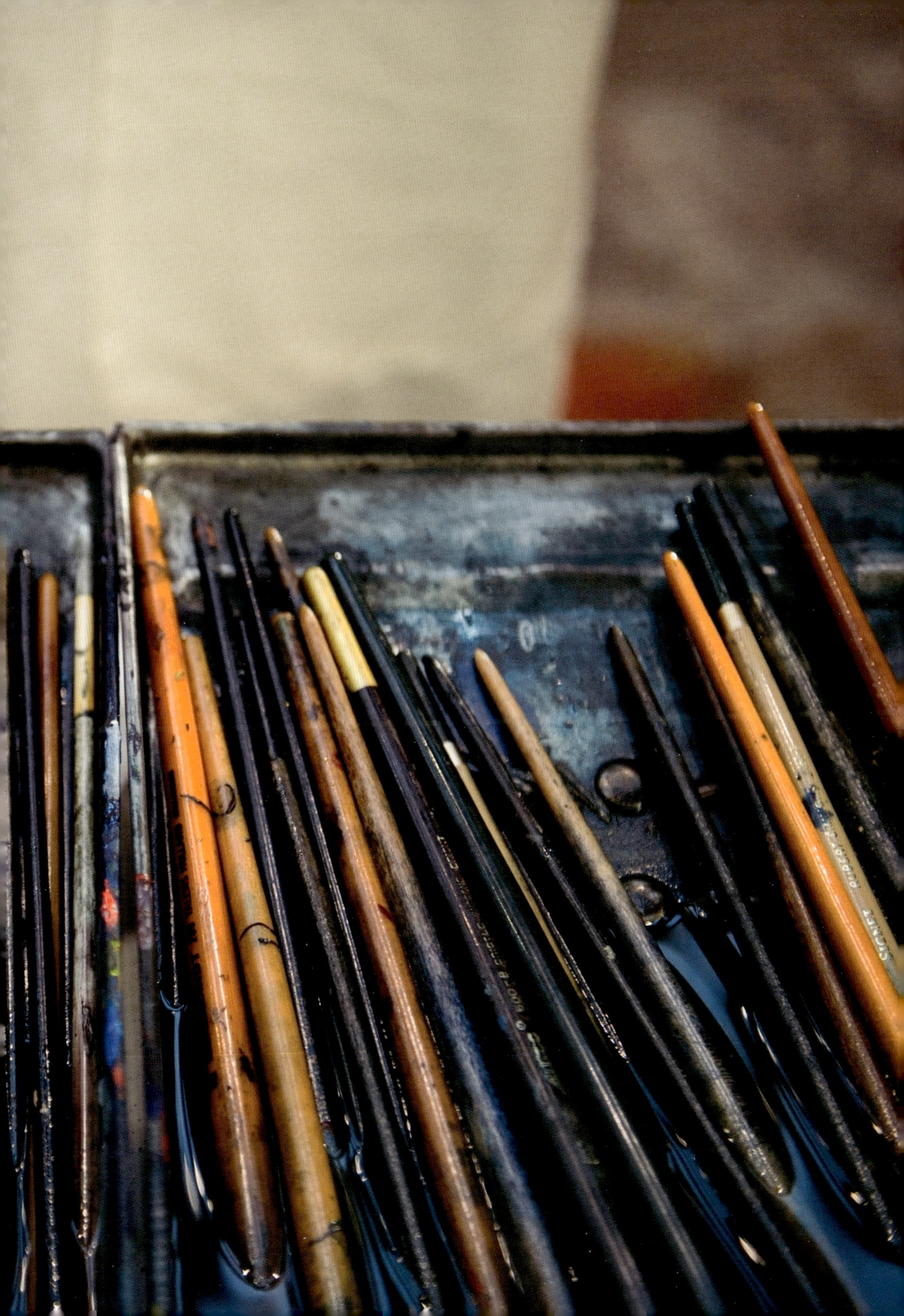

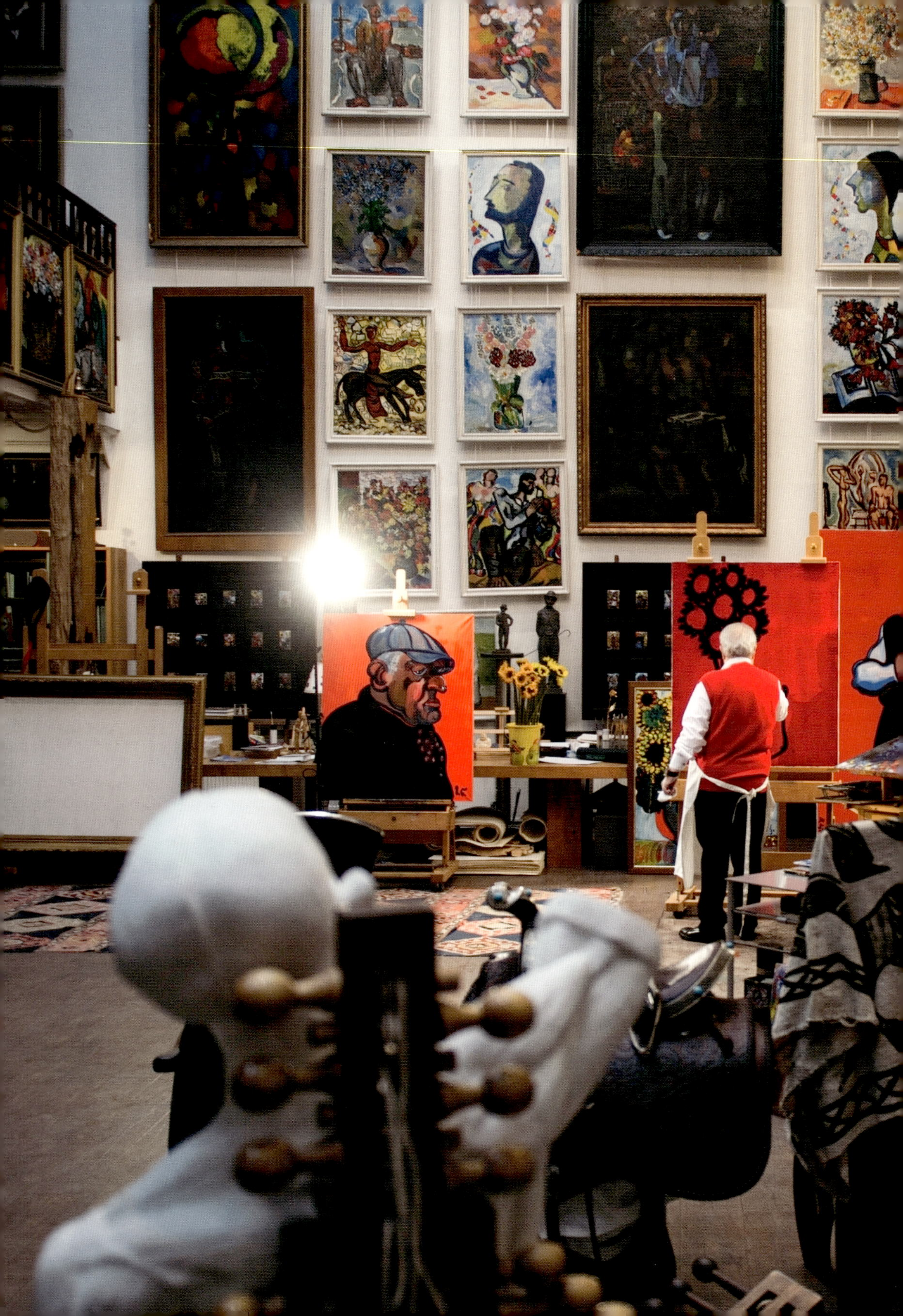

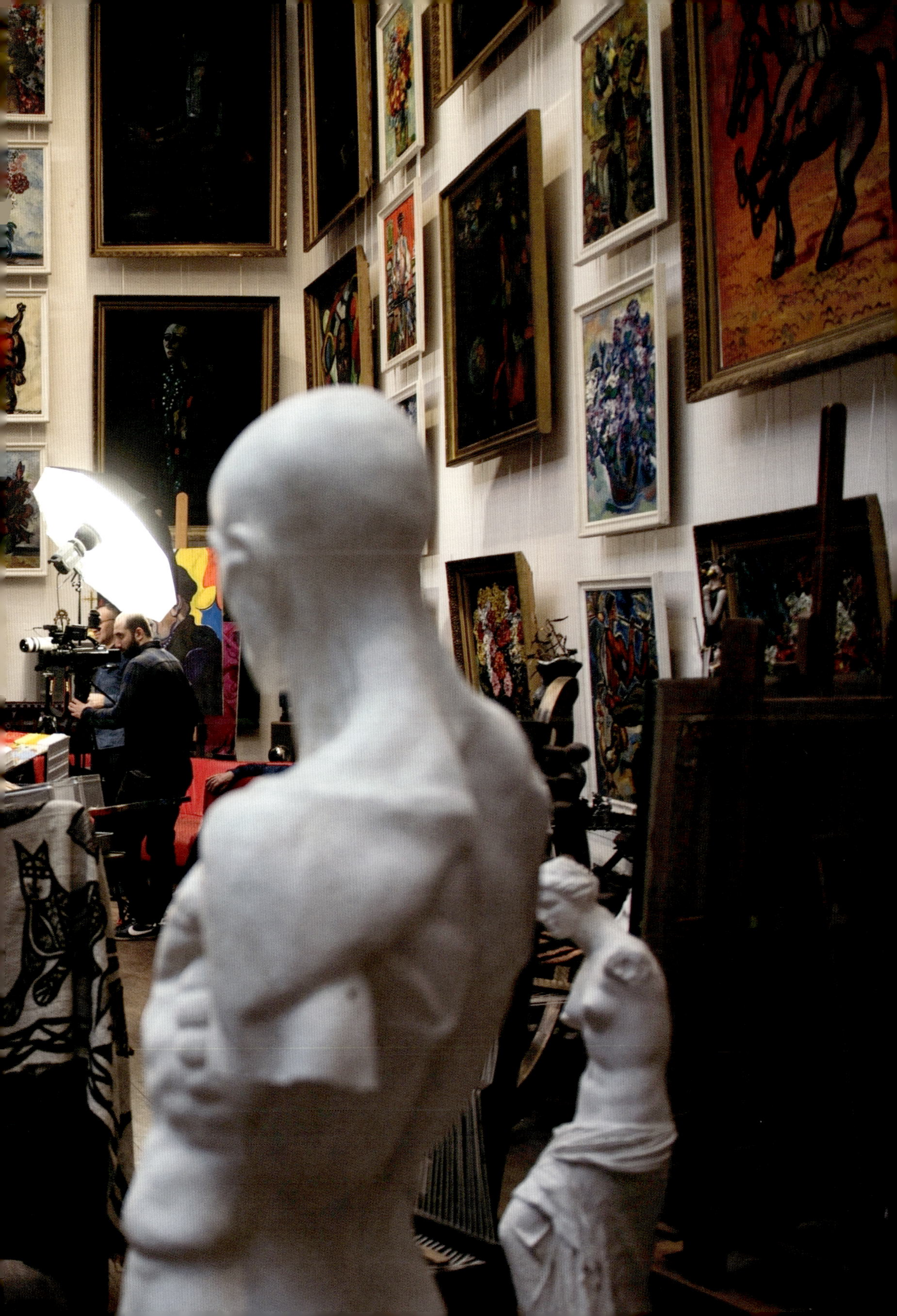

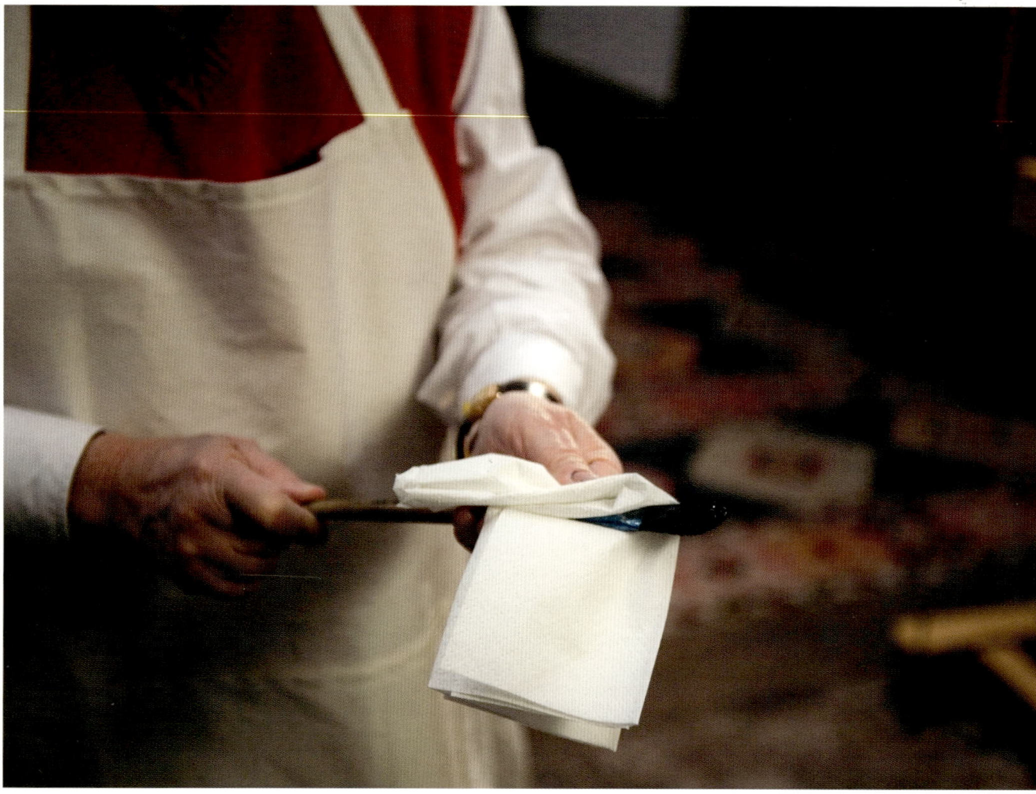

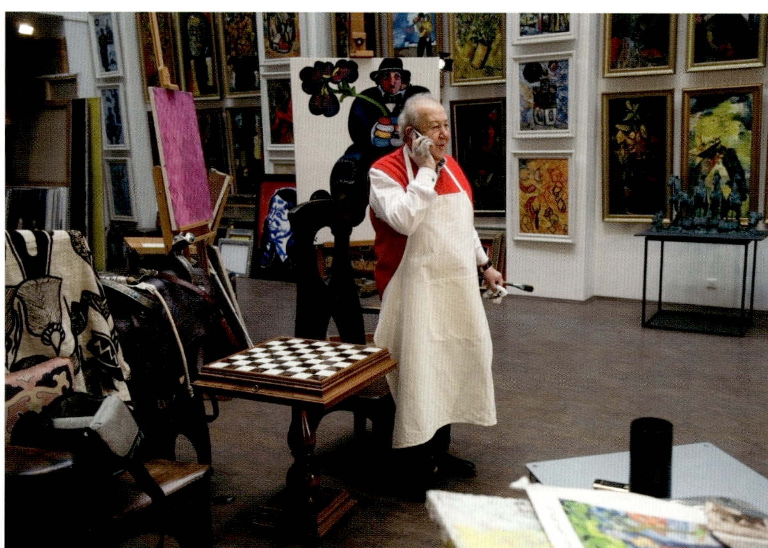

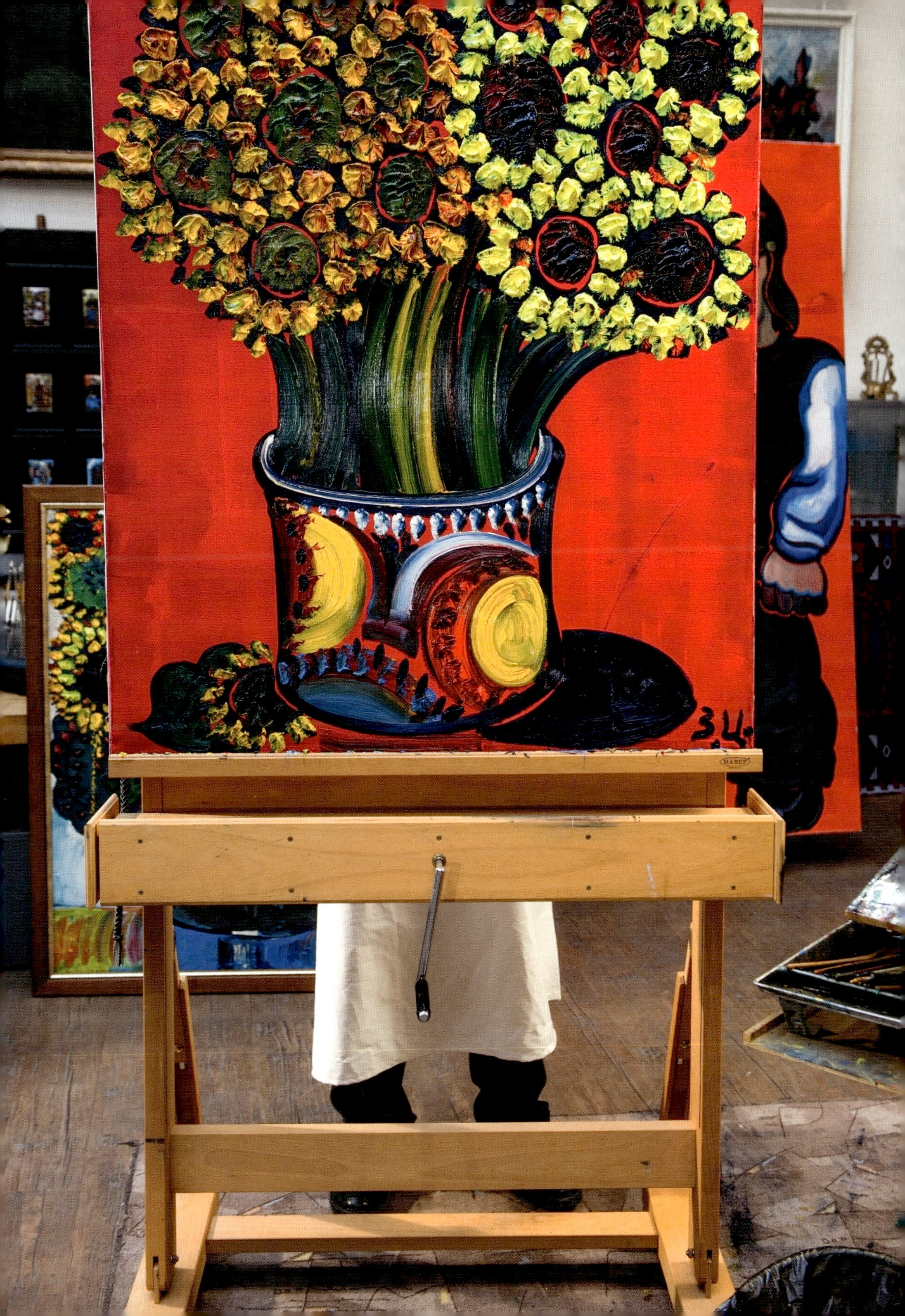

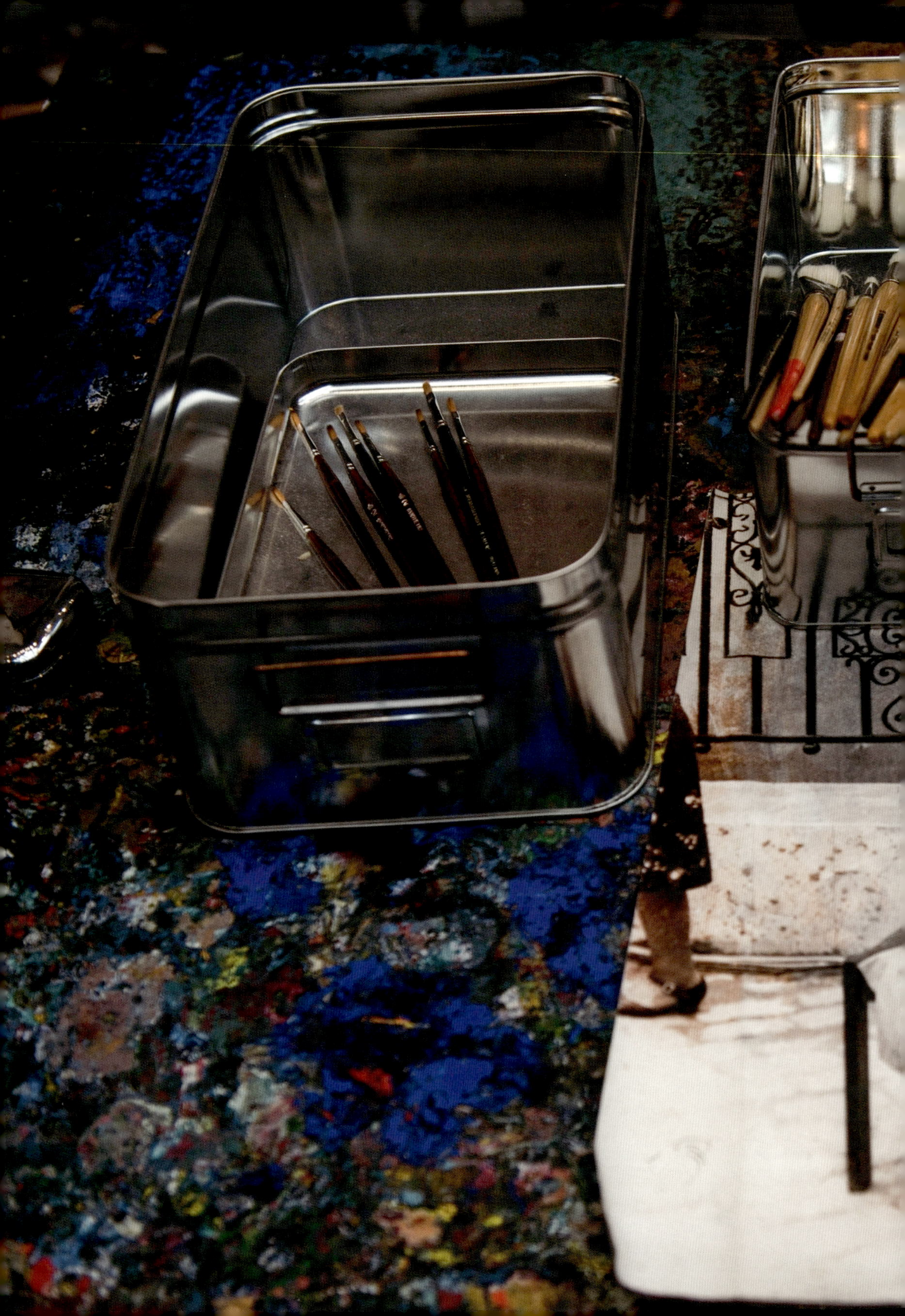

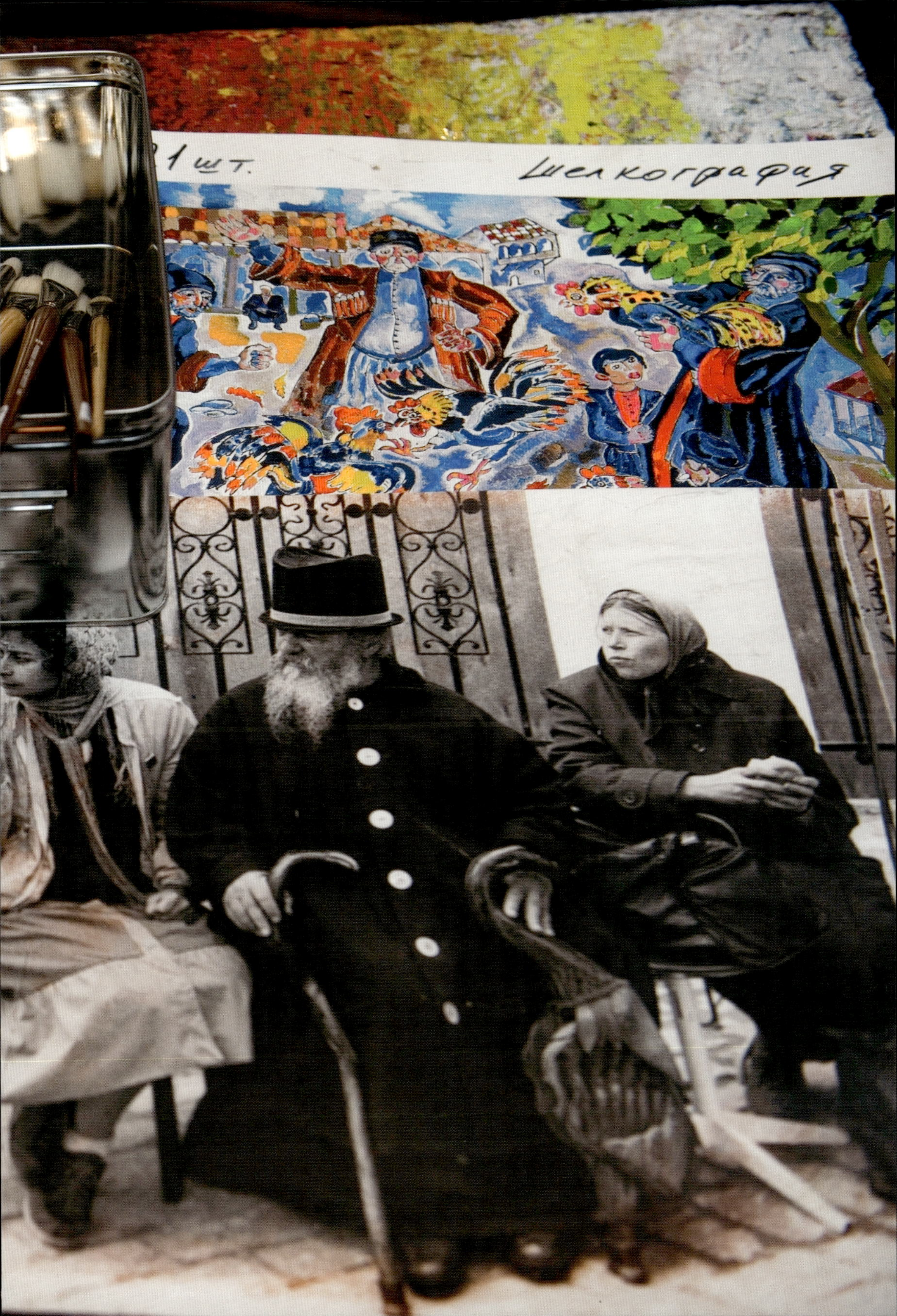
Шелкография

Peredelkino
Moscow

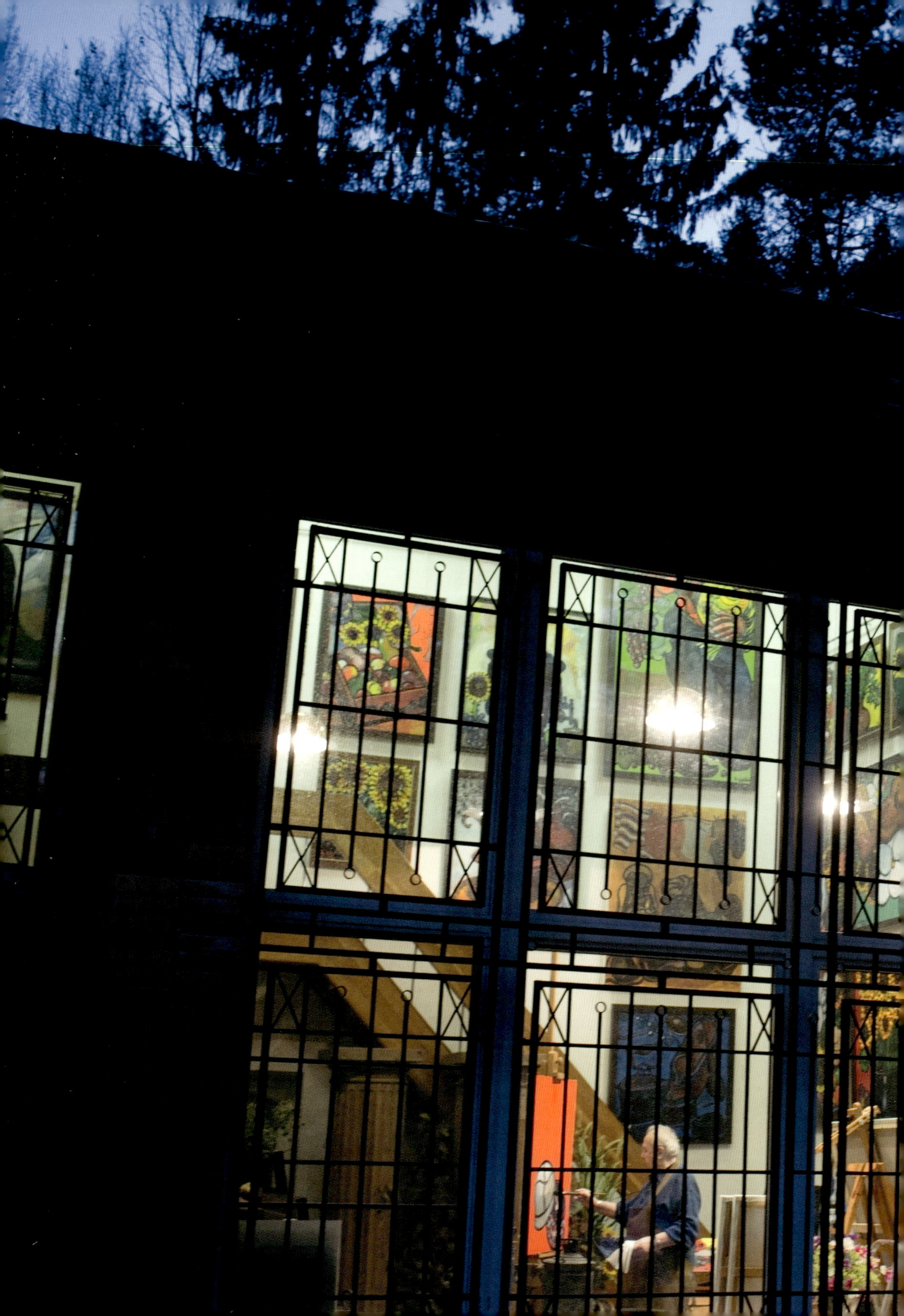

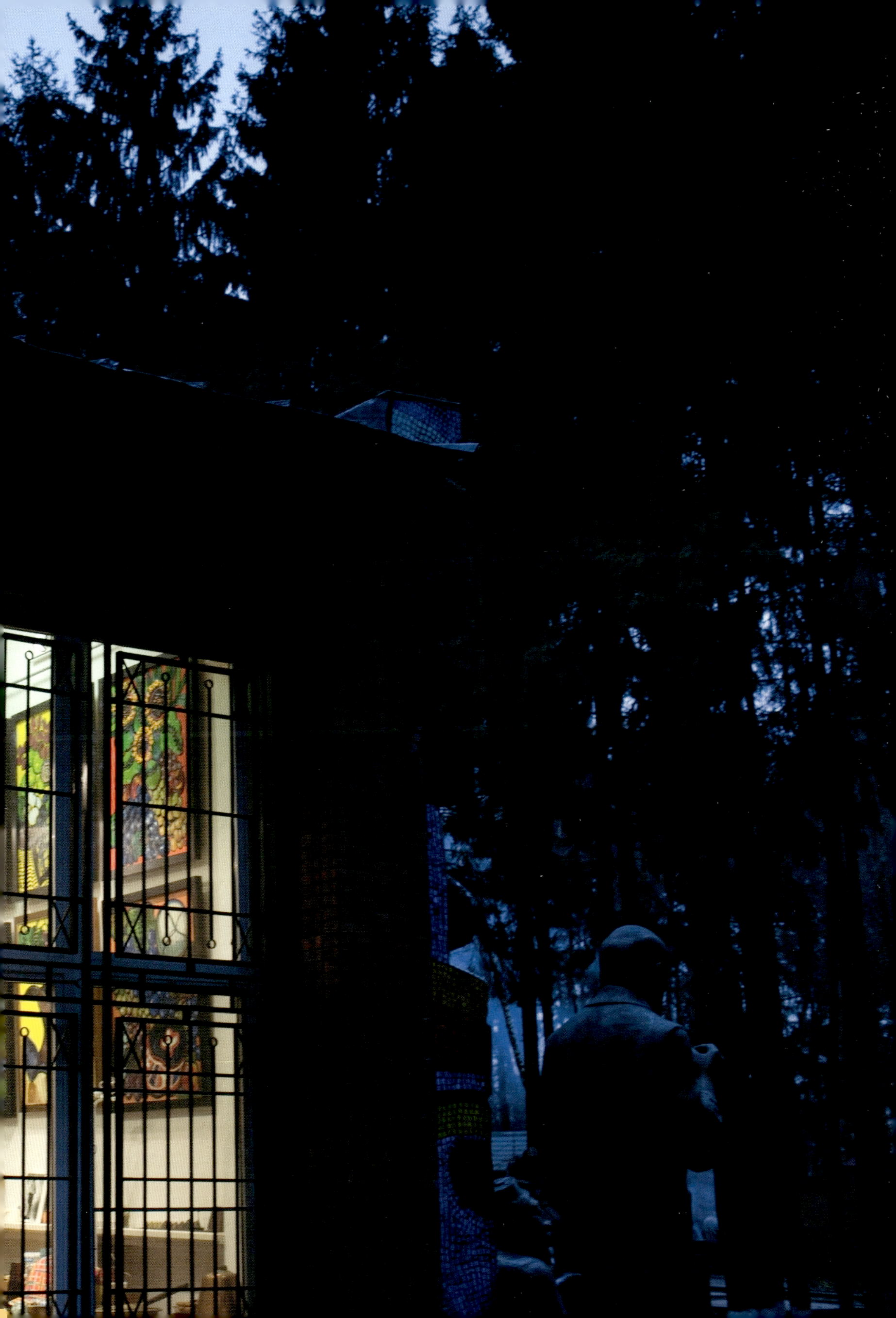

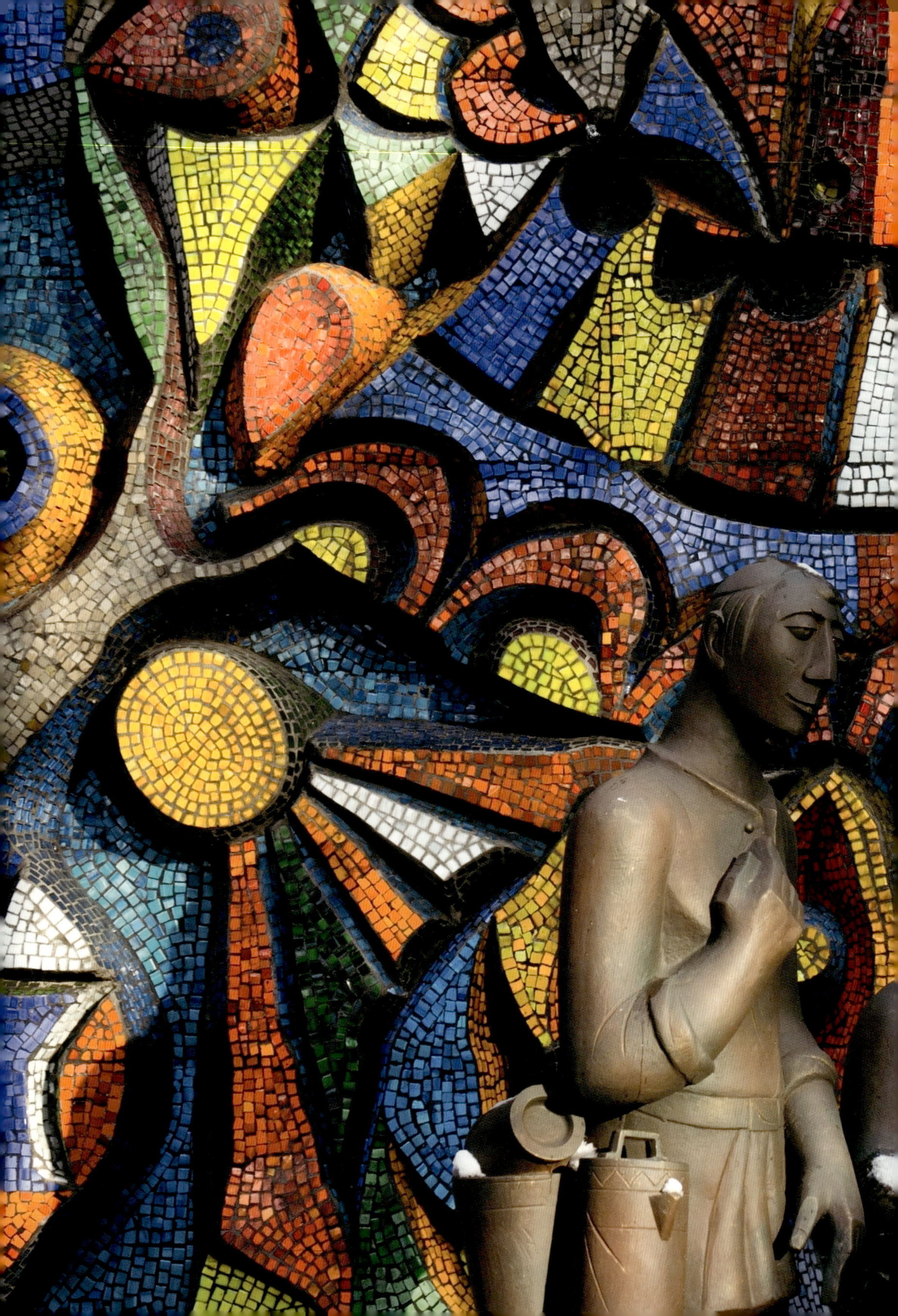

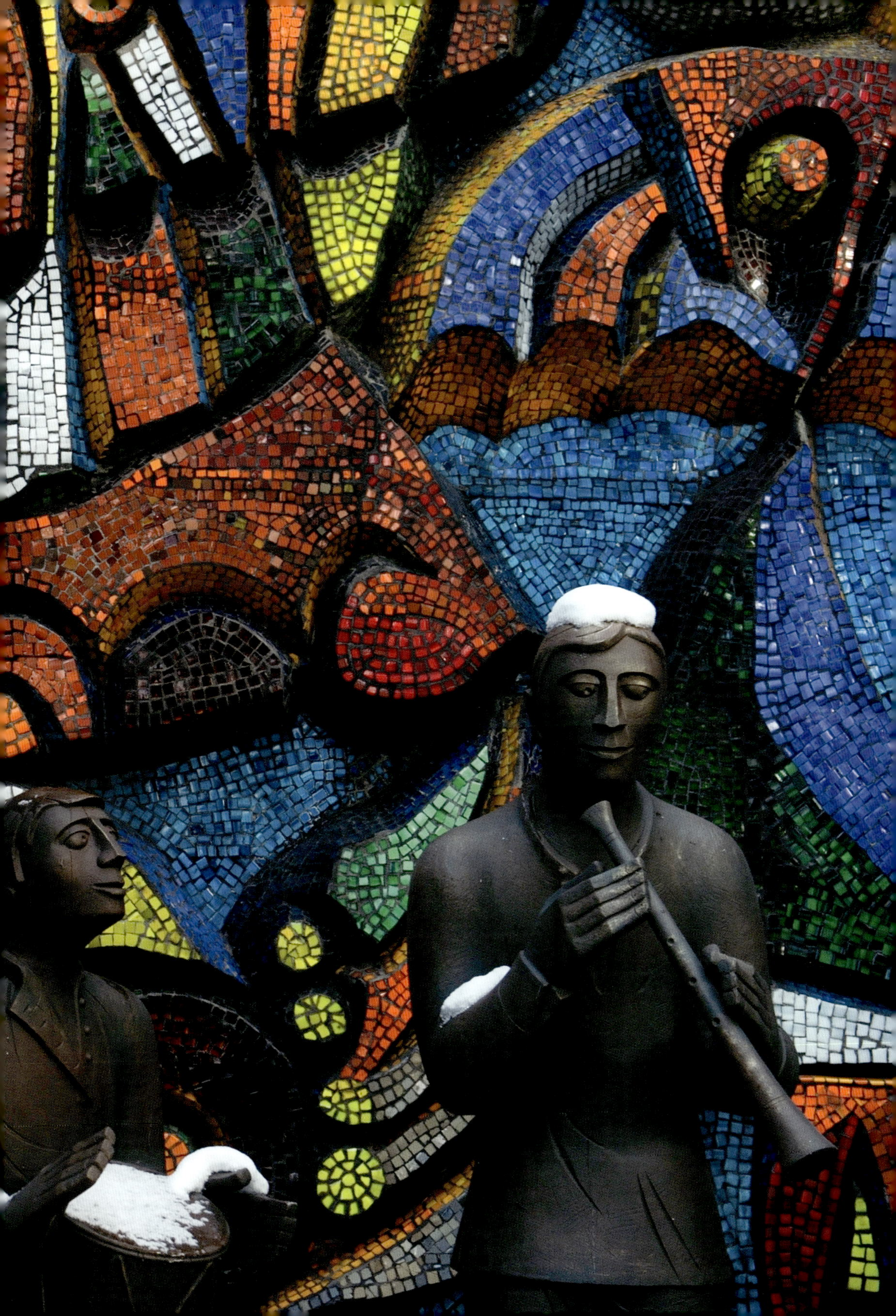

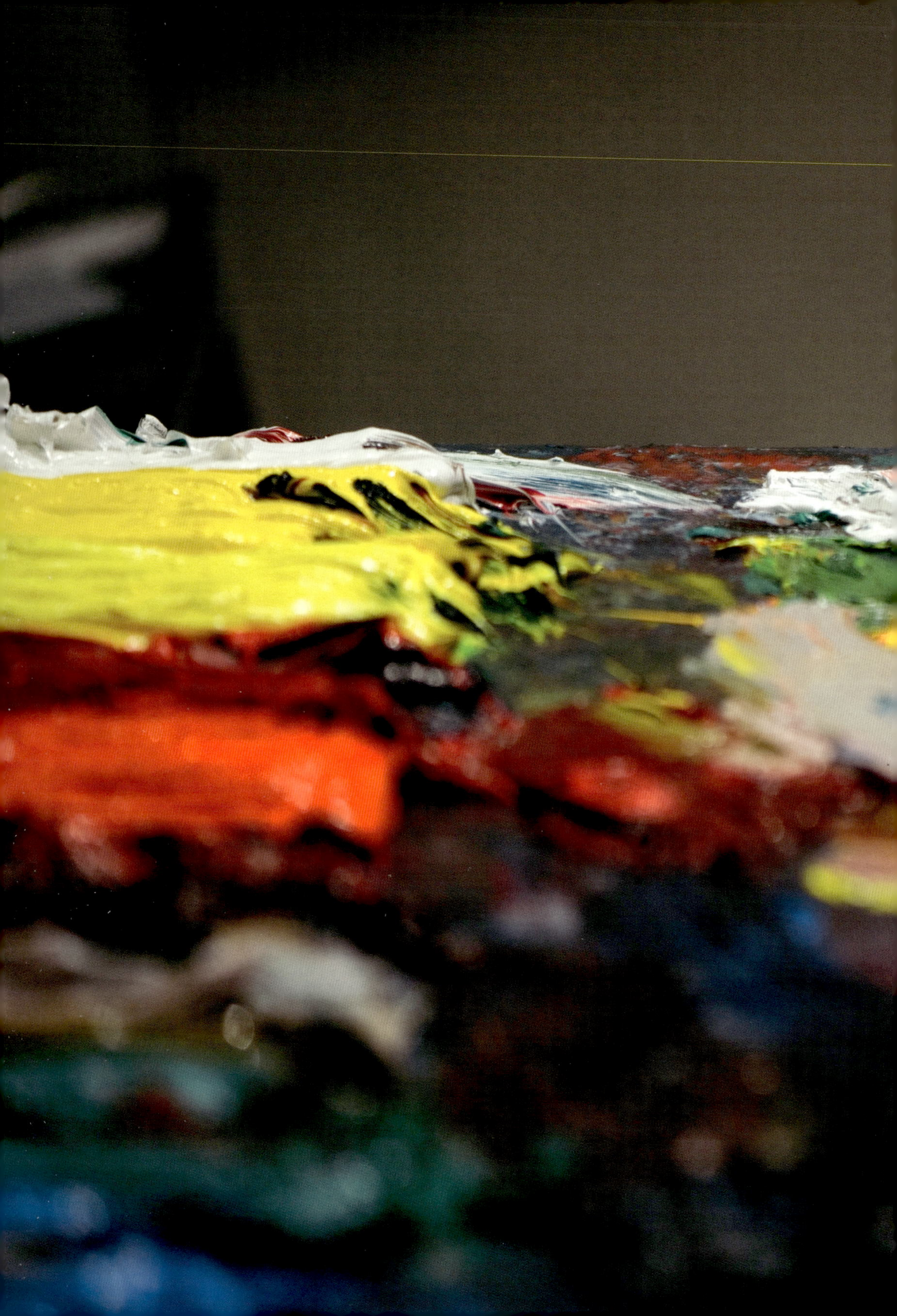

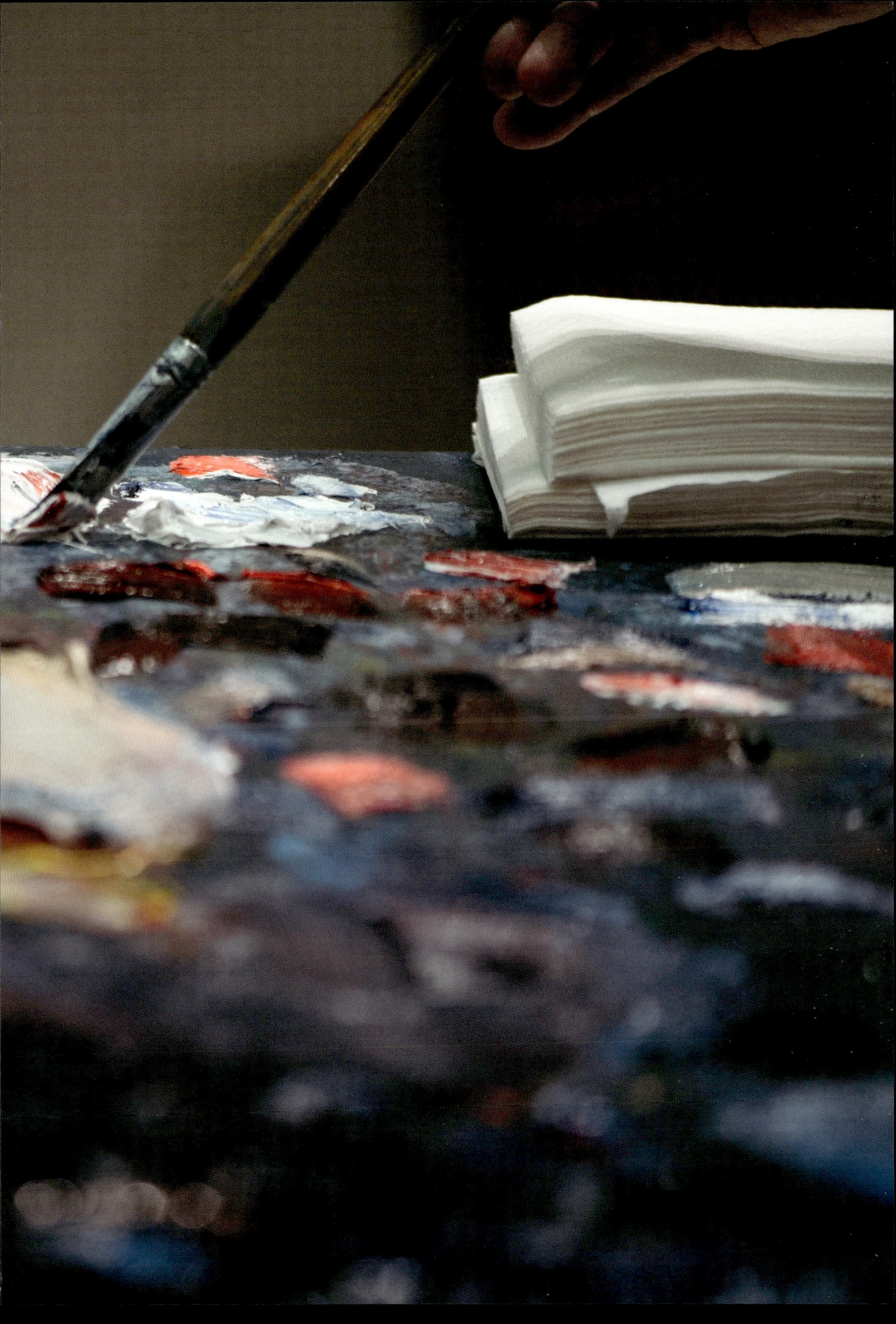

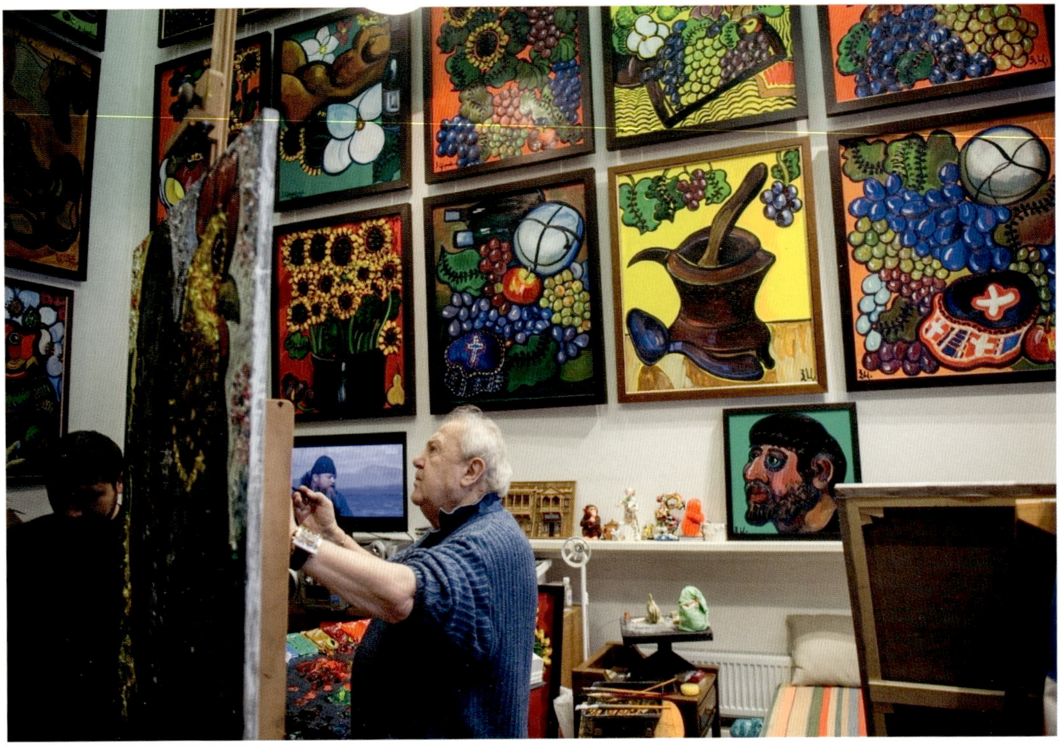

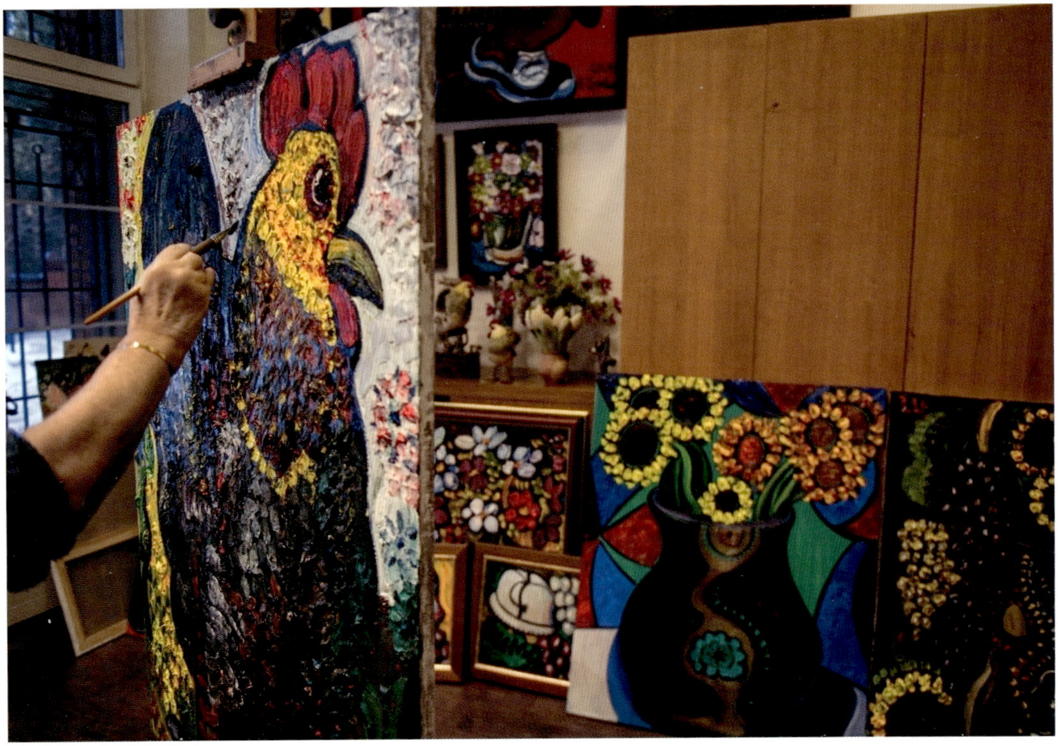

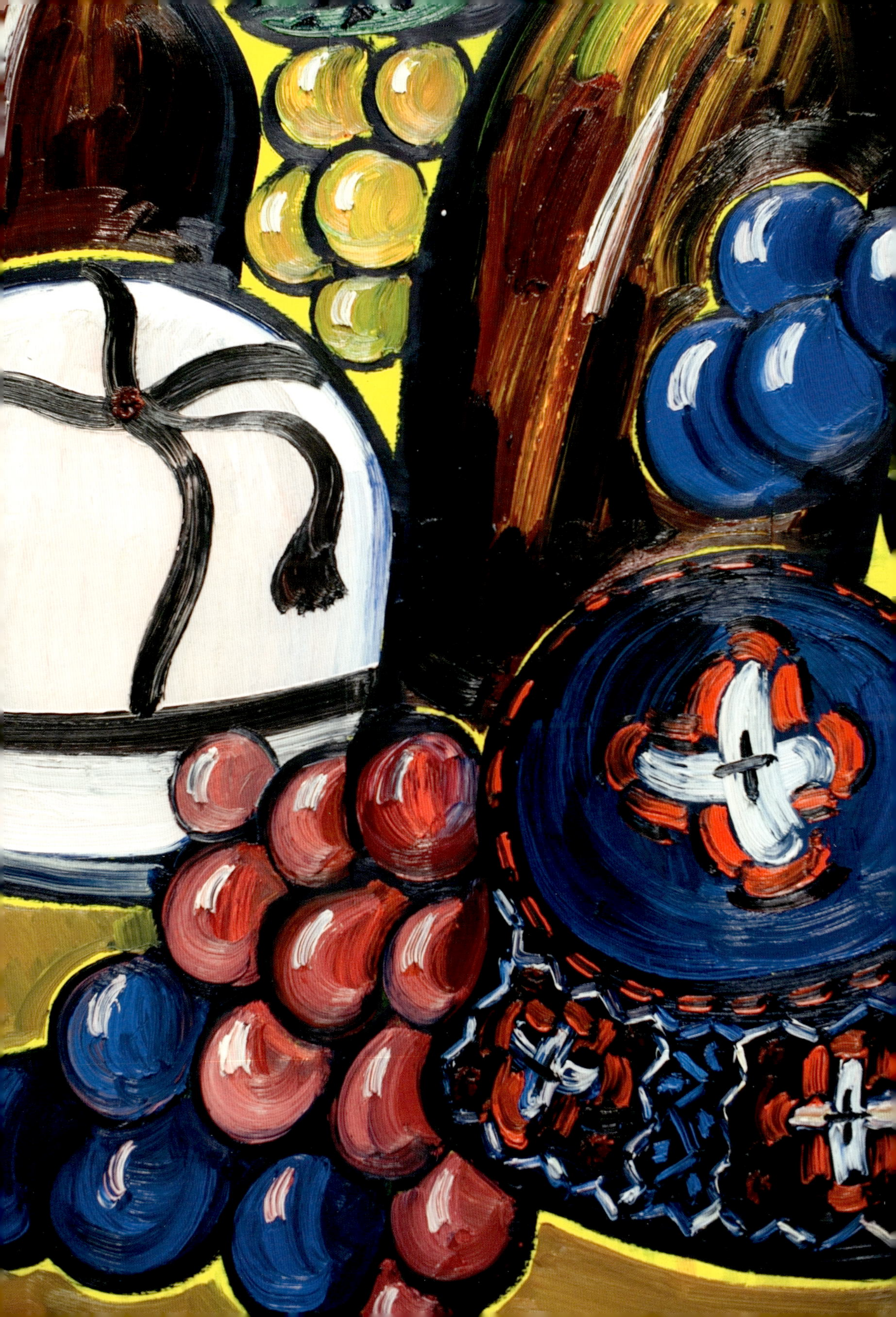

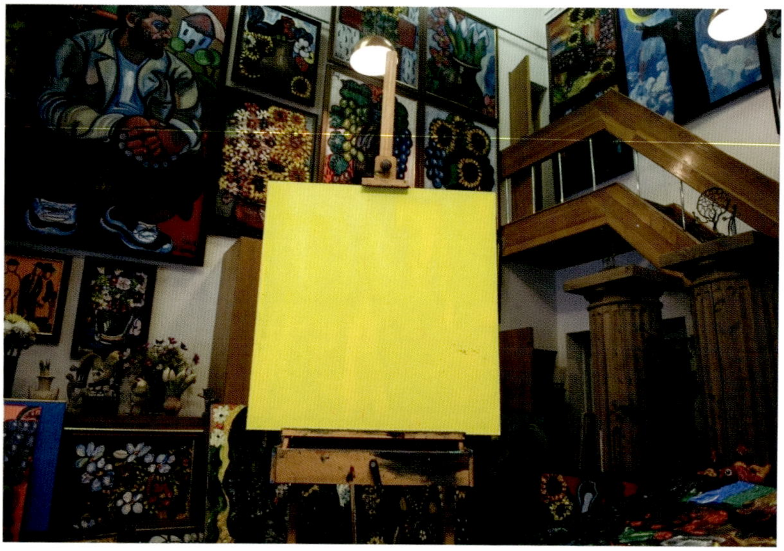

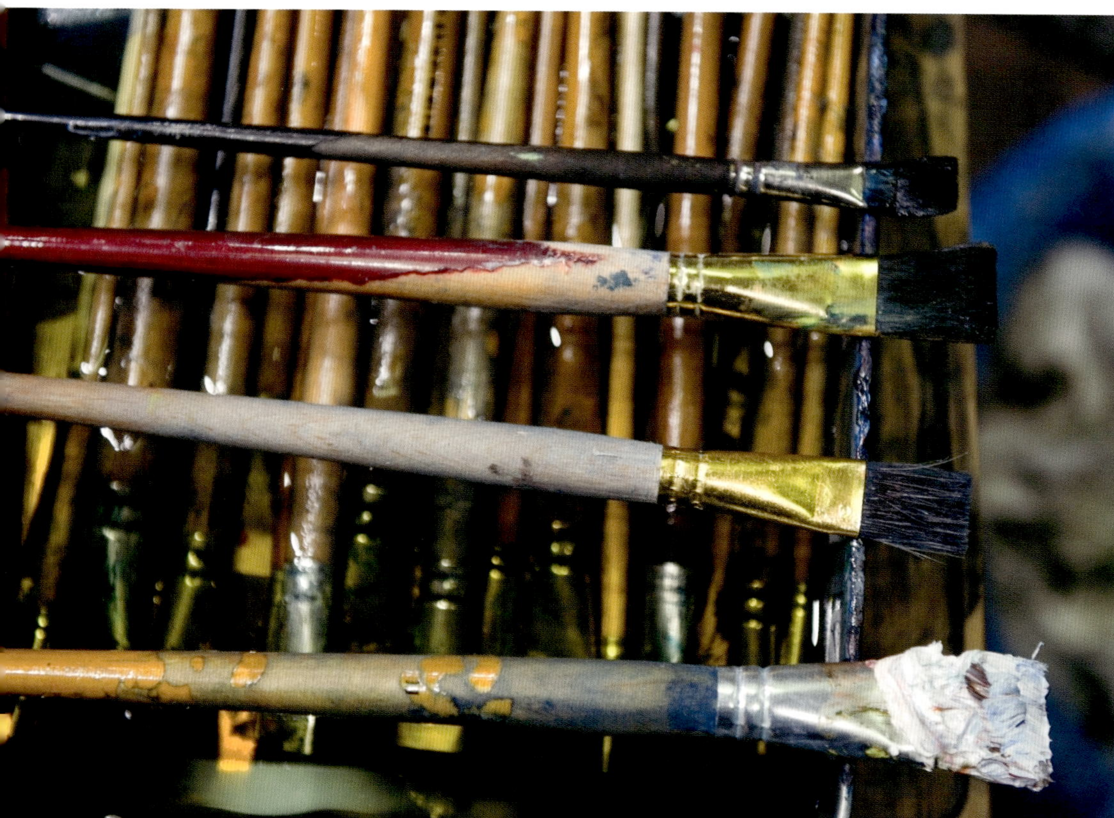

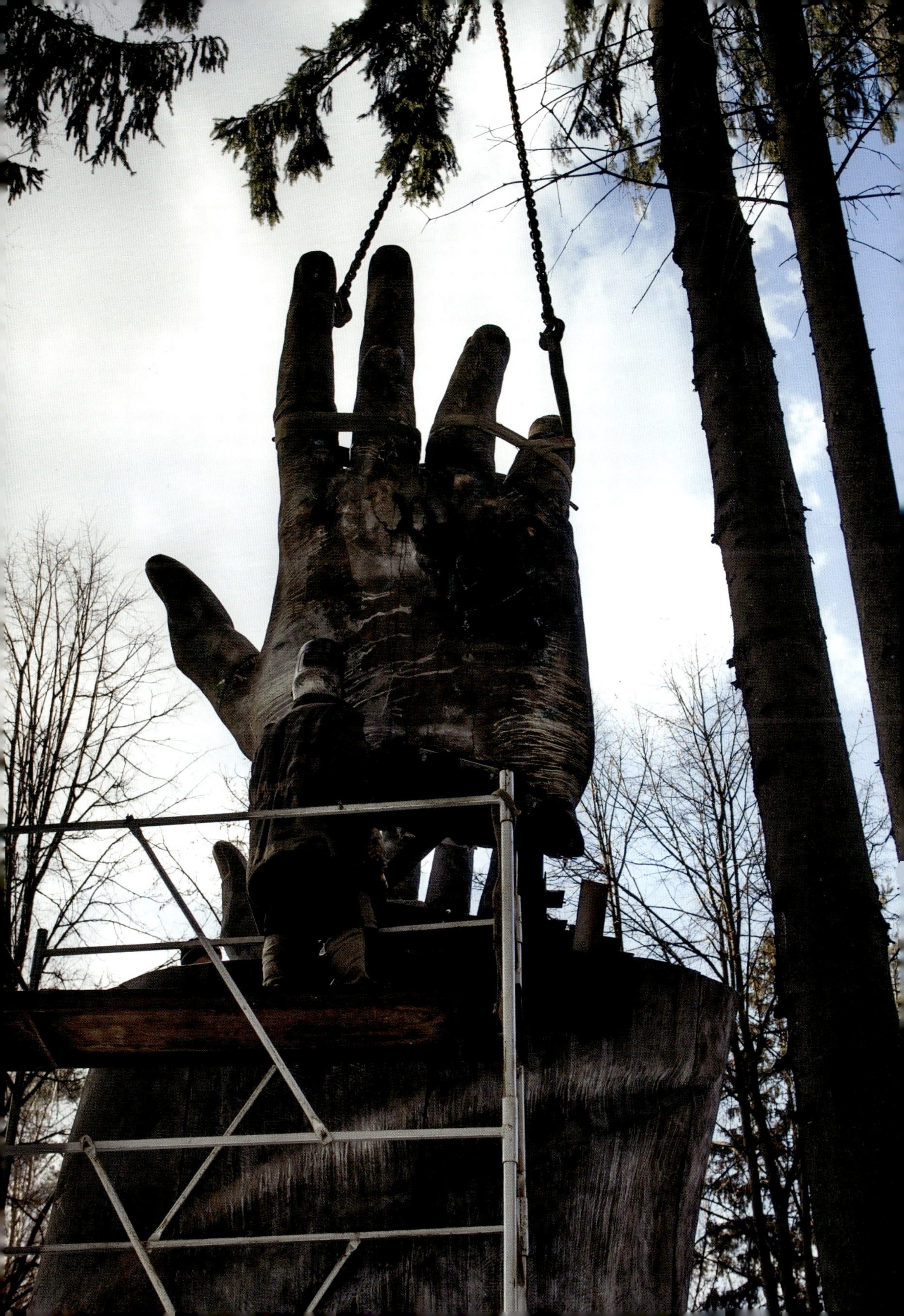

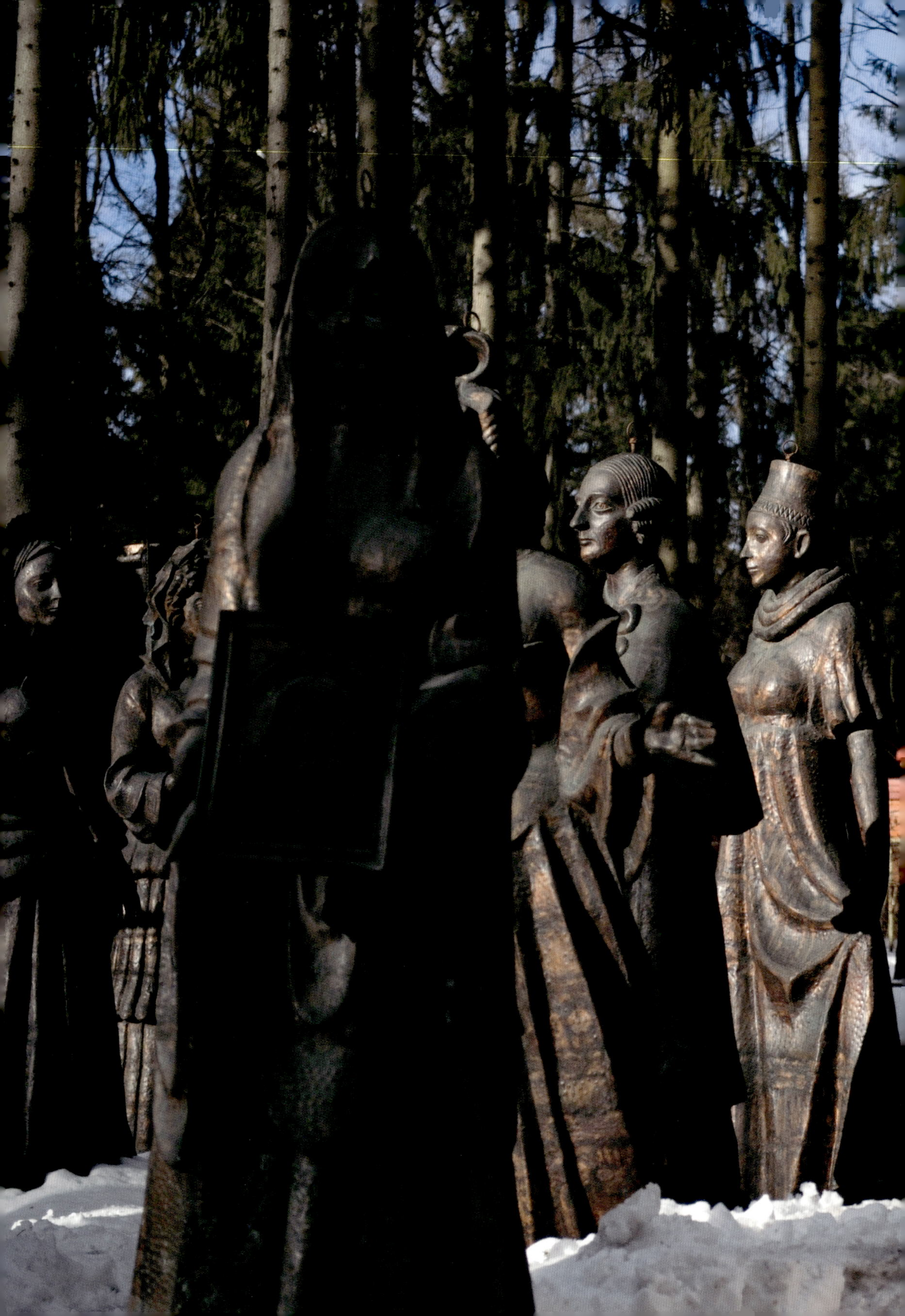

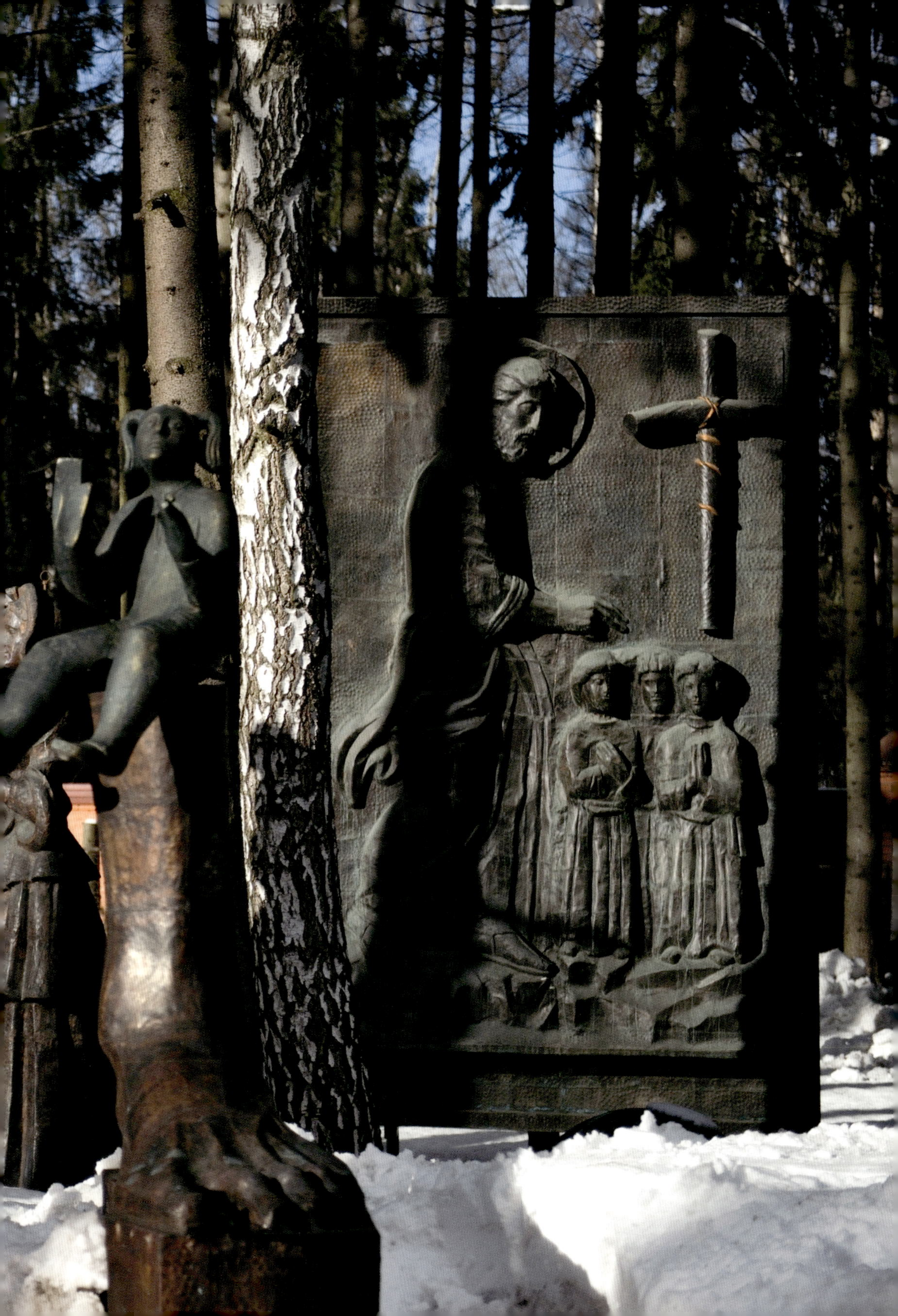

New York

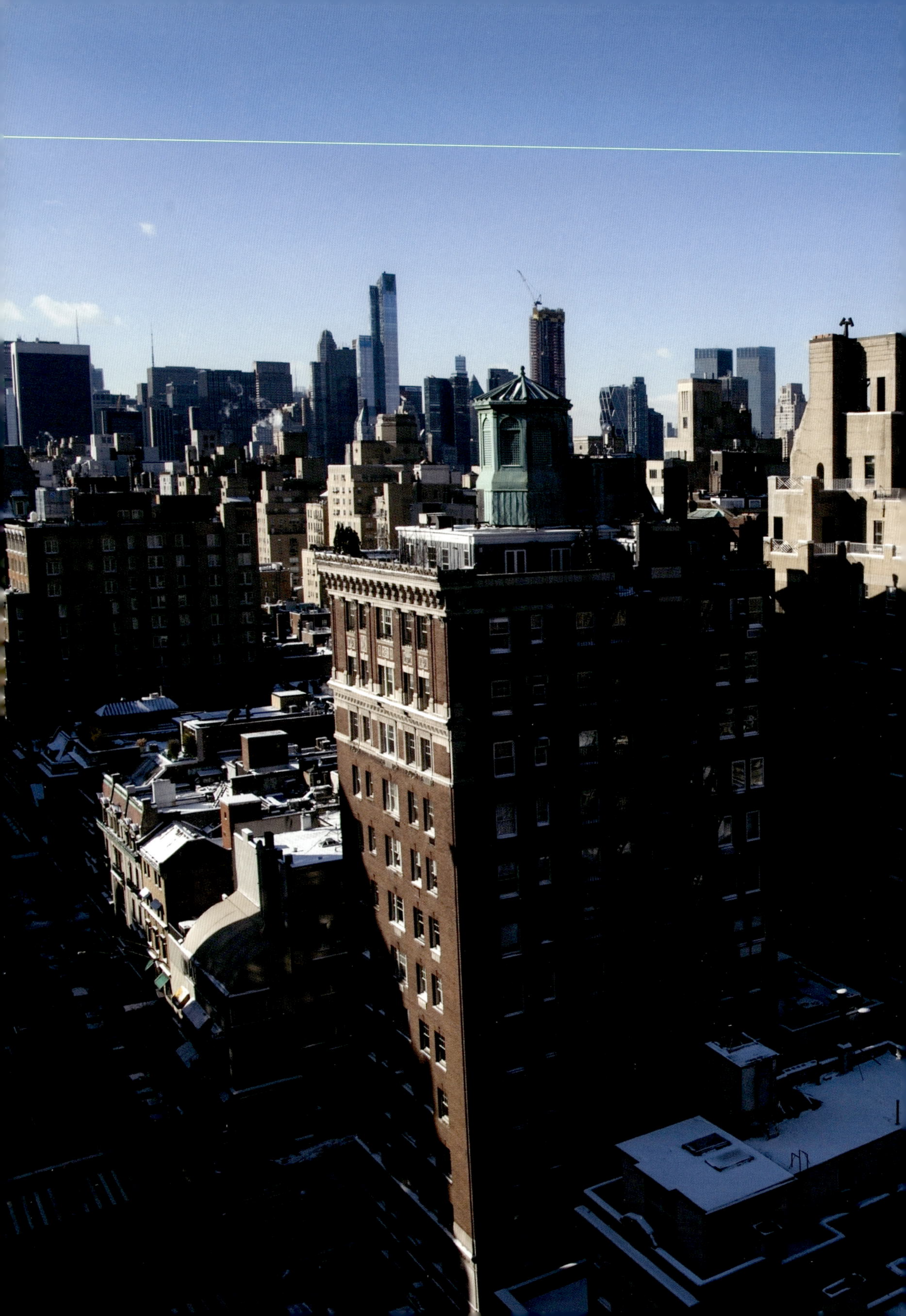

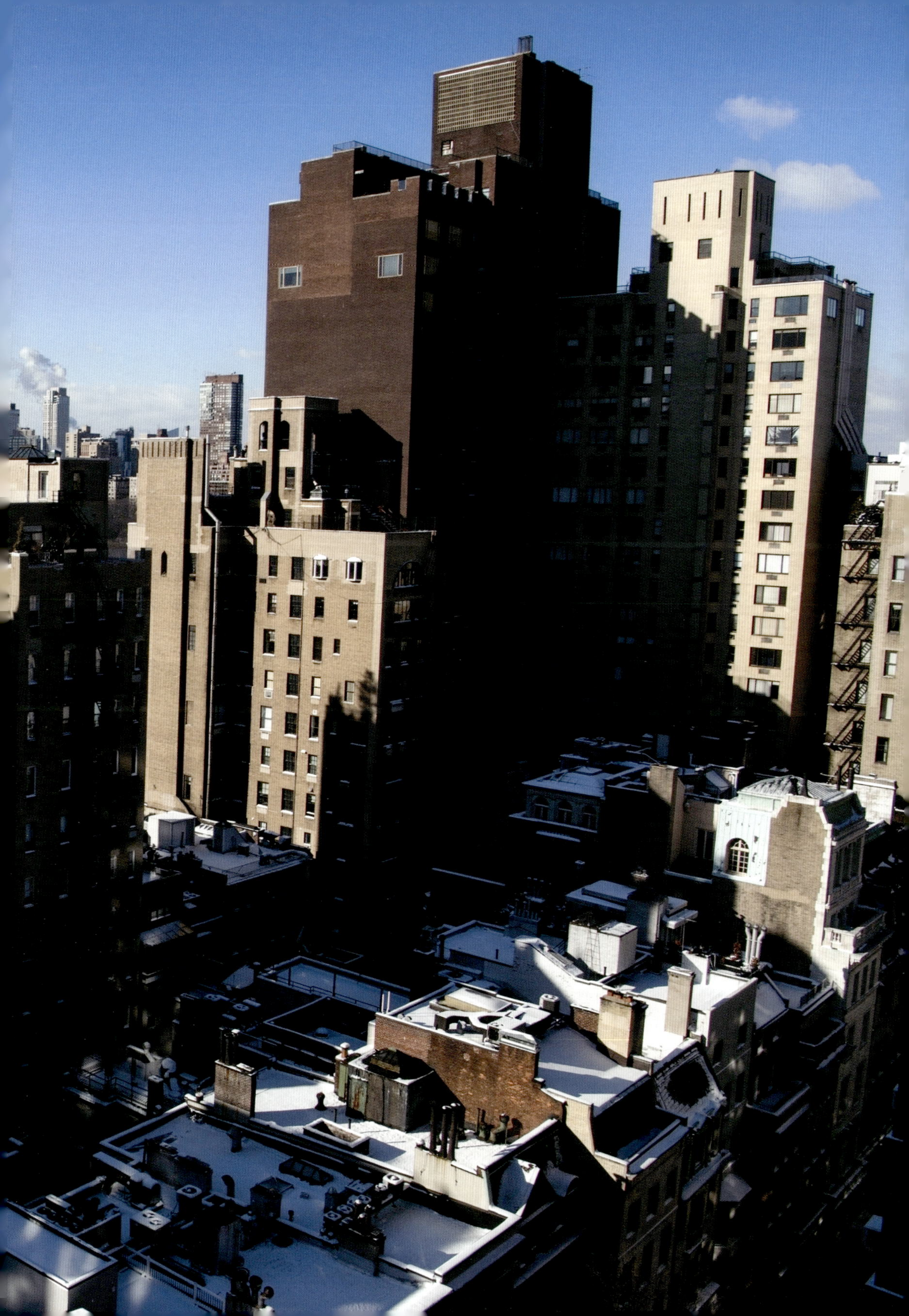

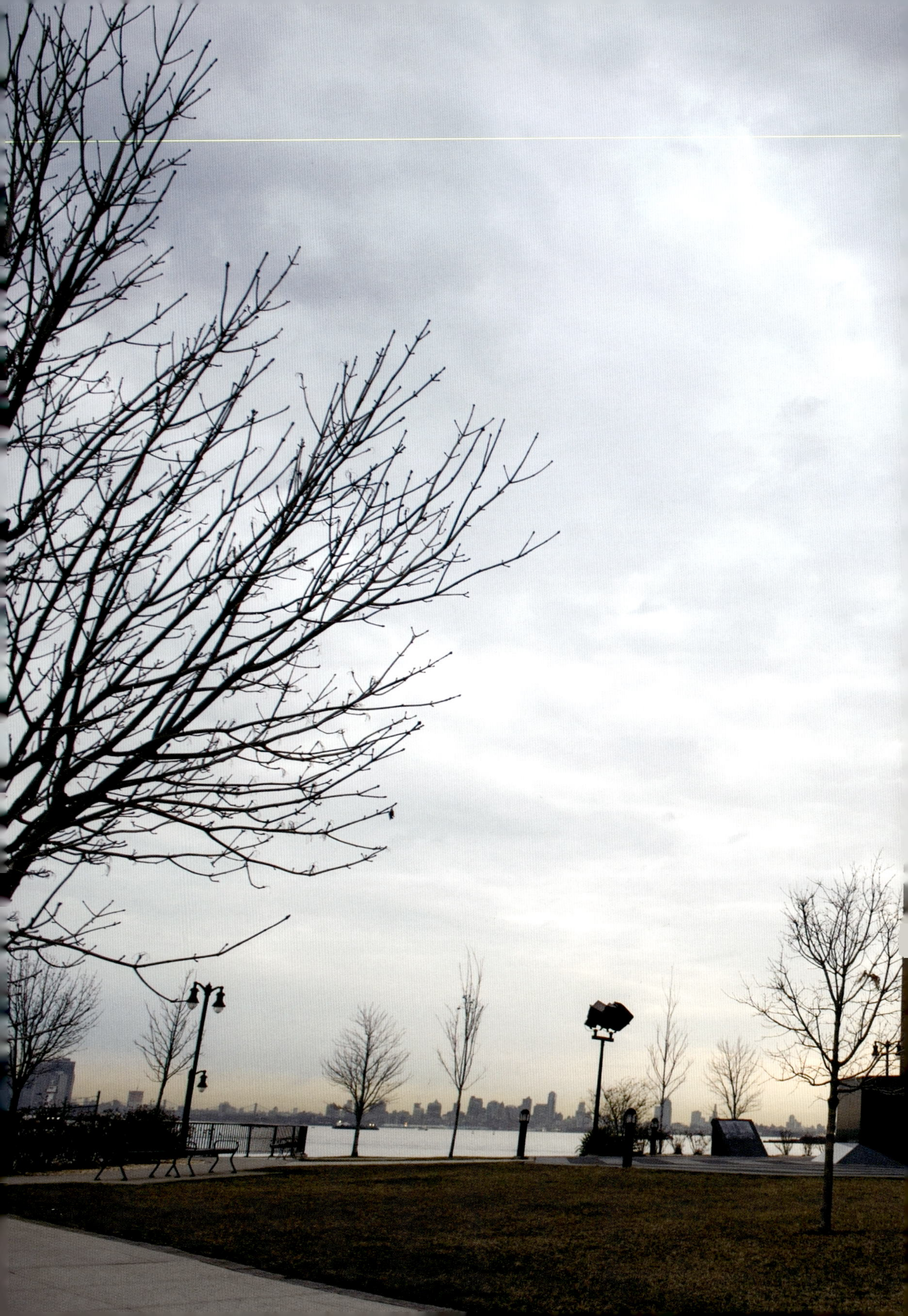

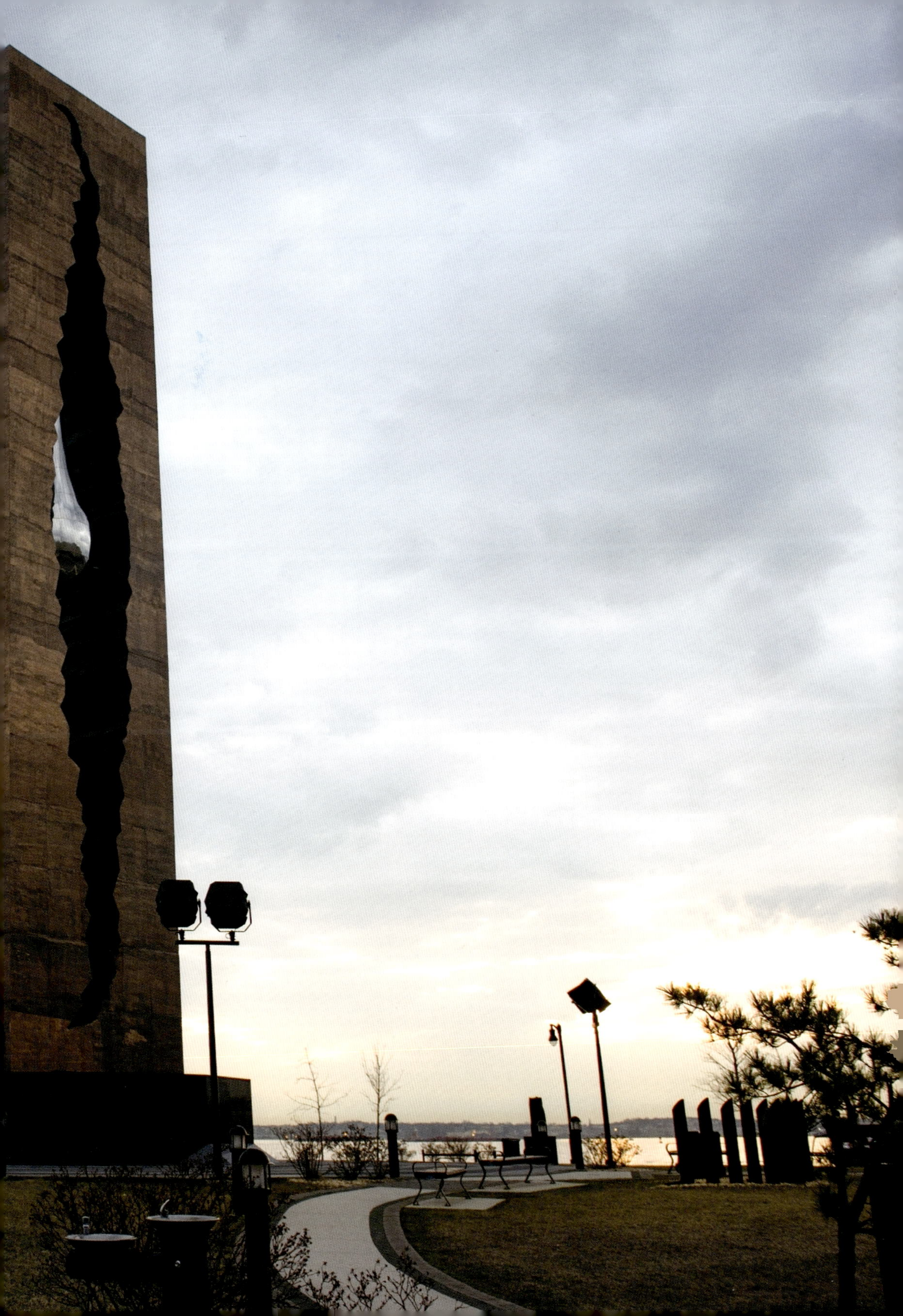

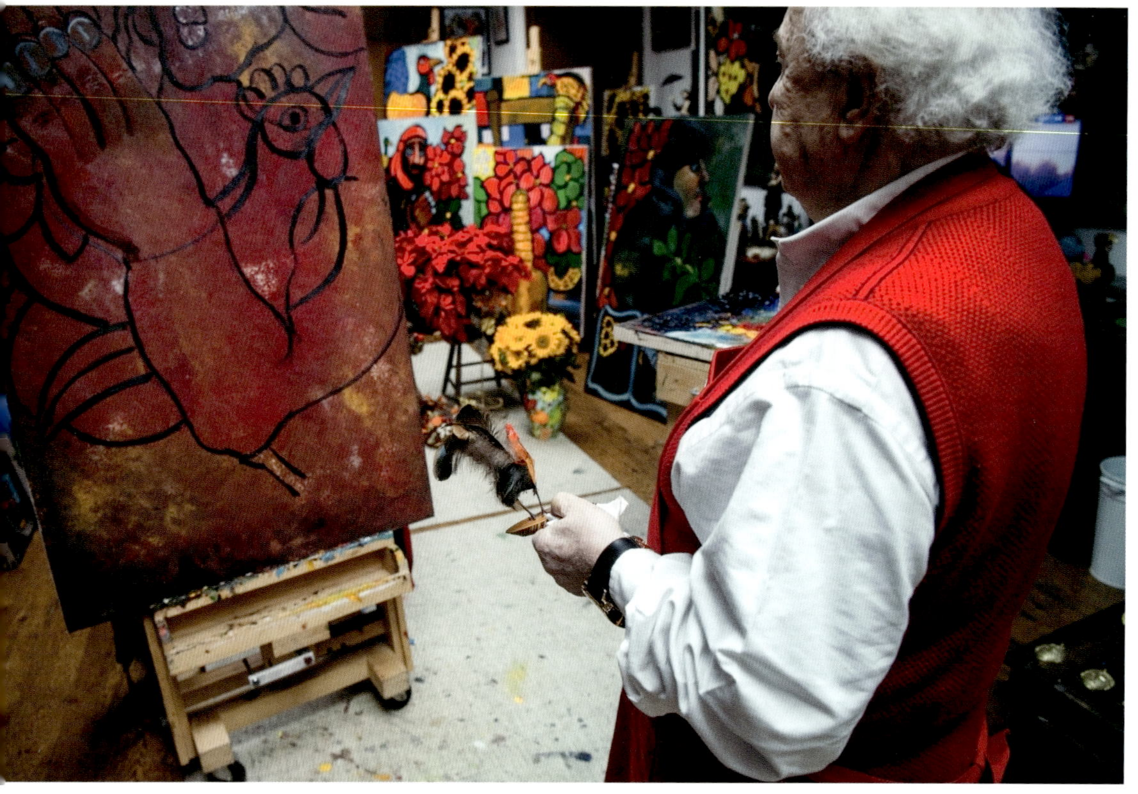

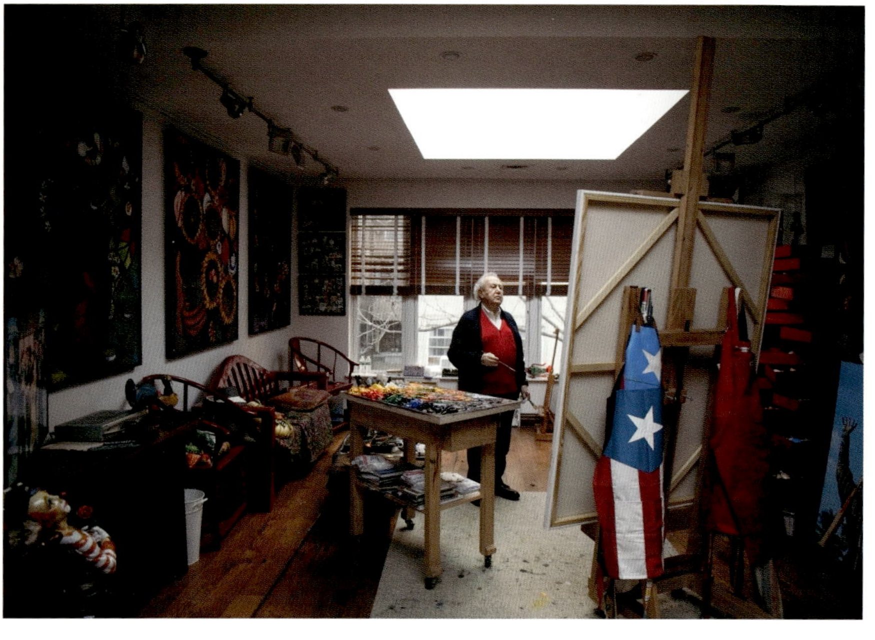

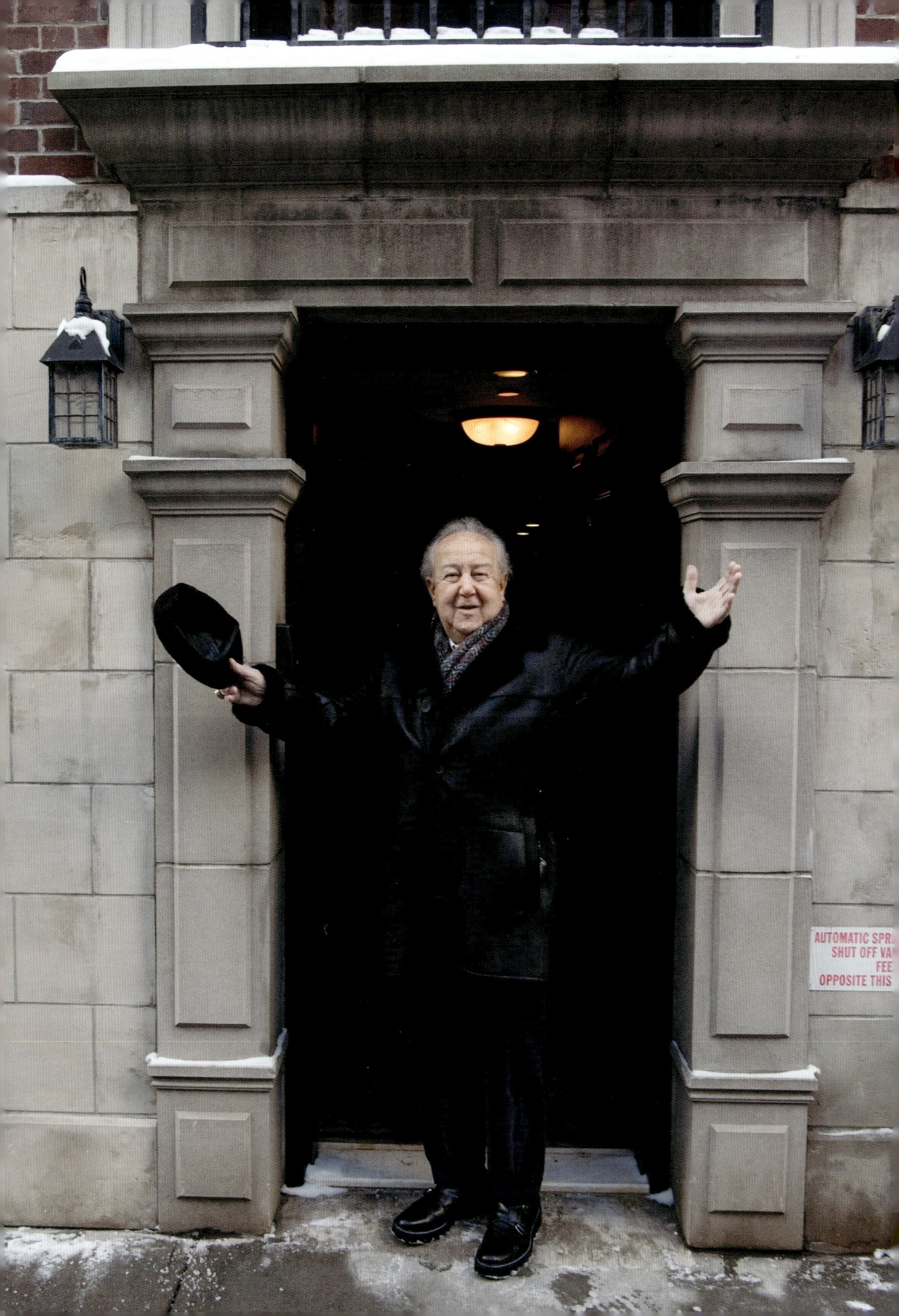
AUTOMATIC SPR
SHUT OFF VA
FEE
OPPOSITE THIS

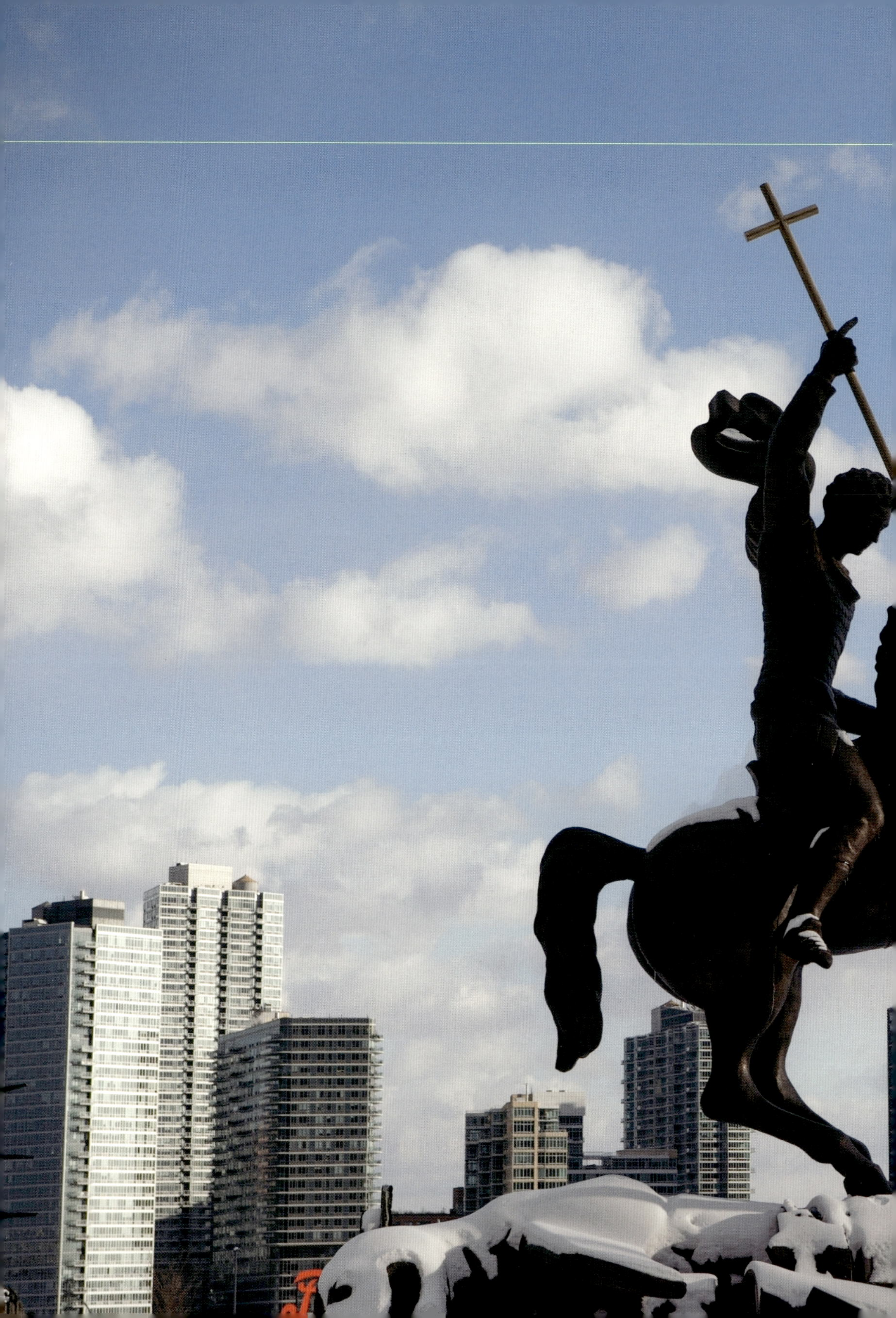

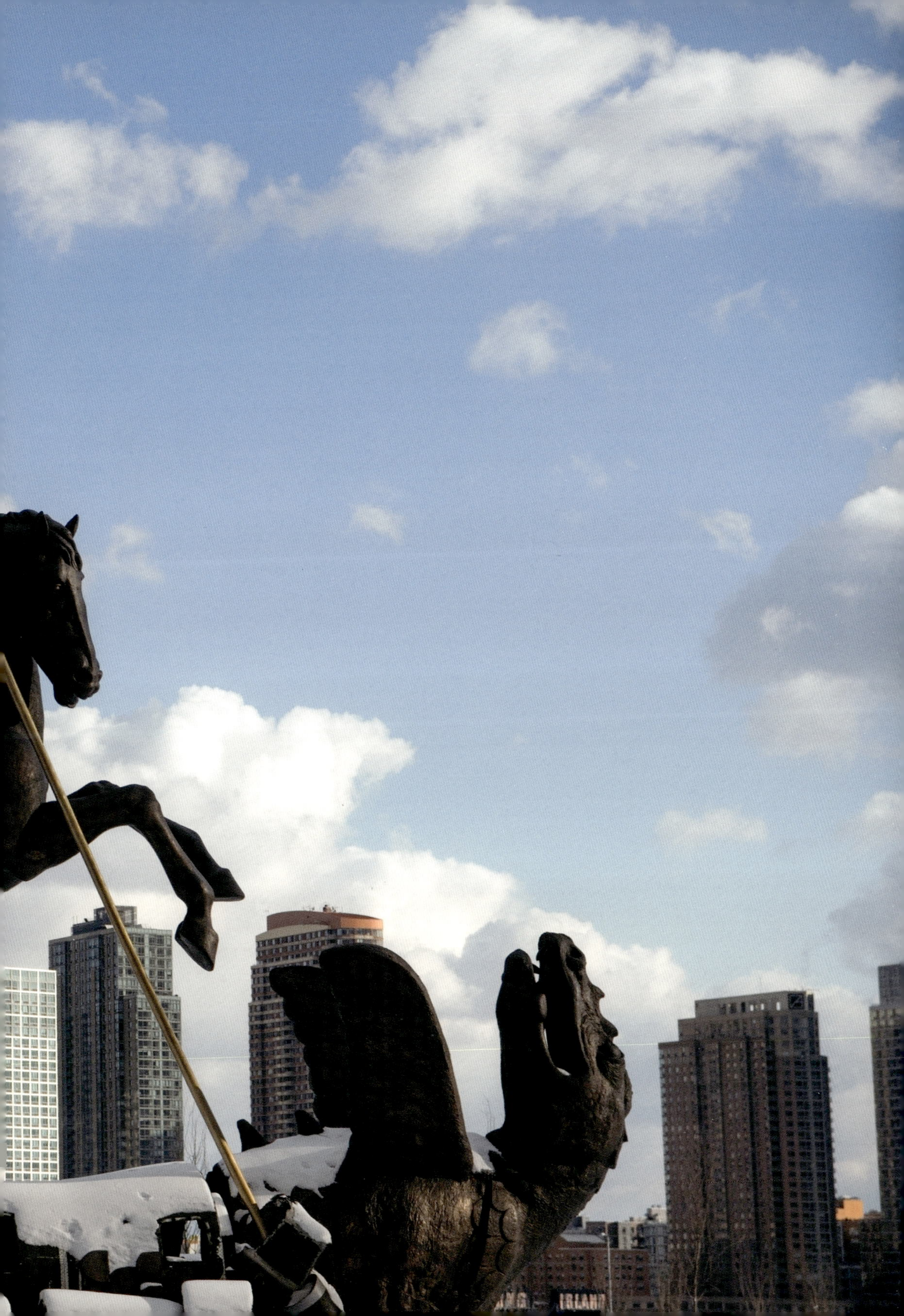

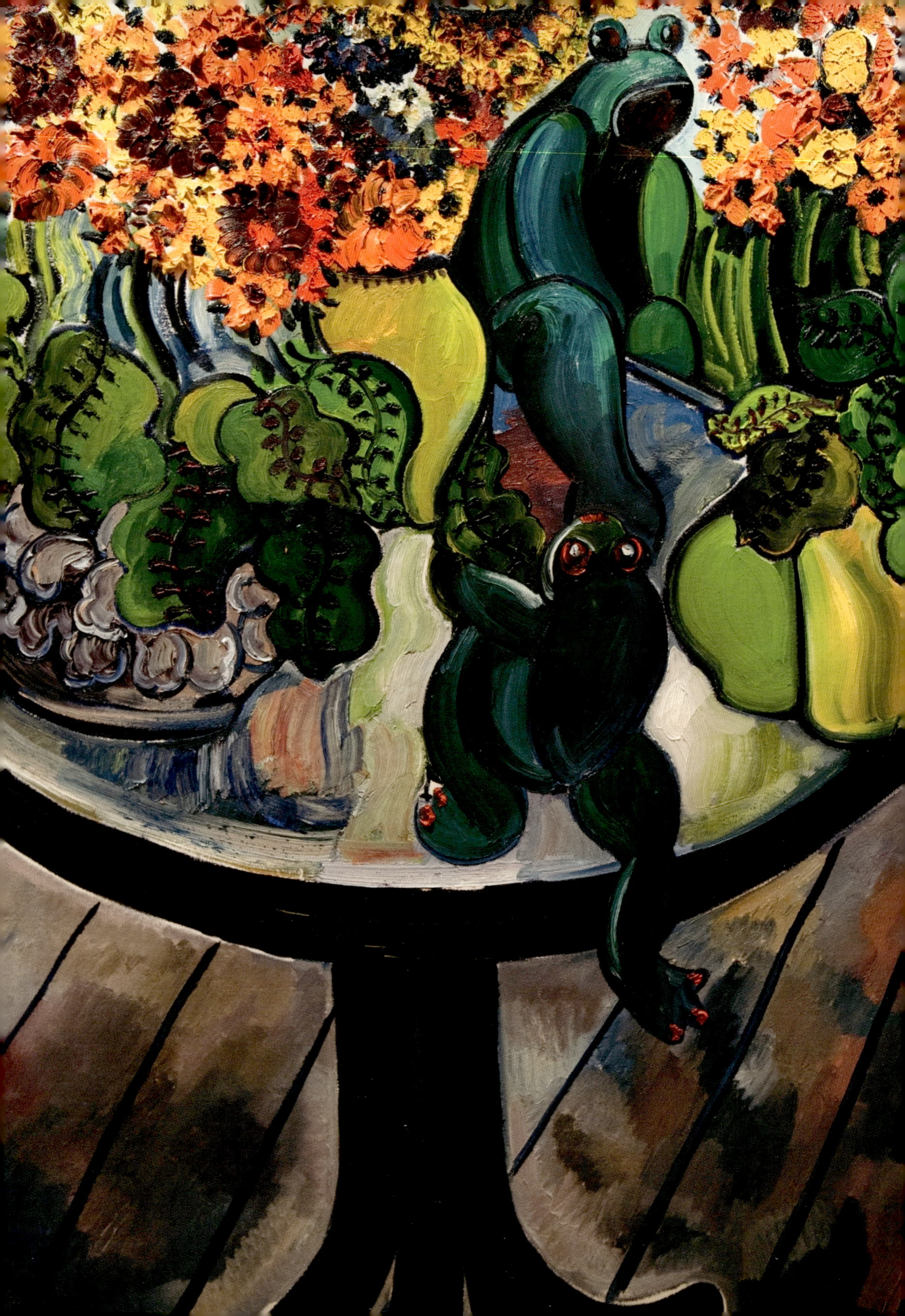

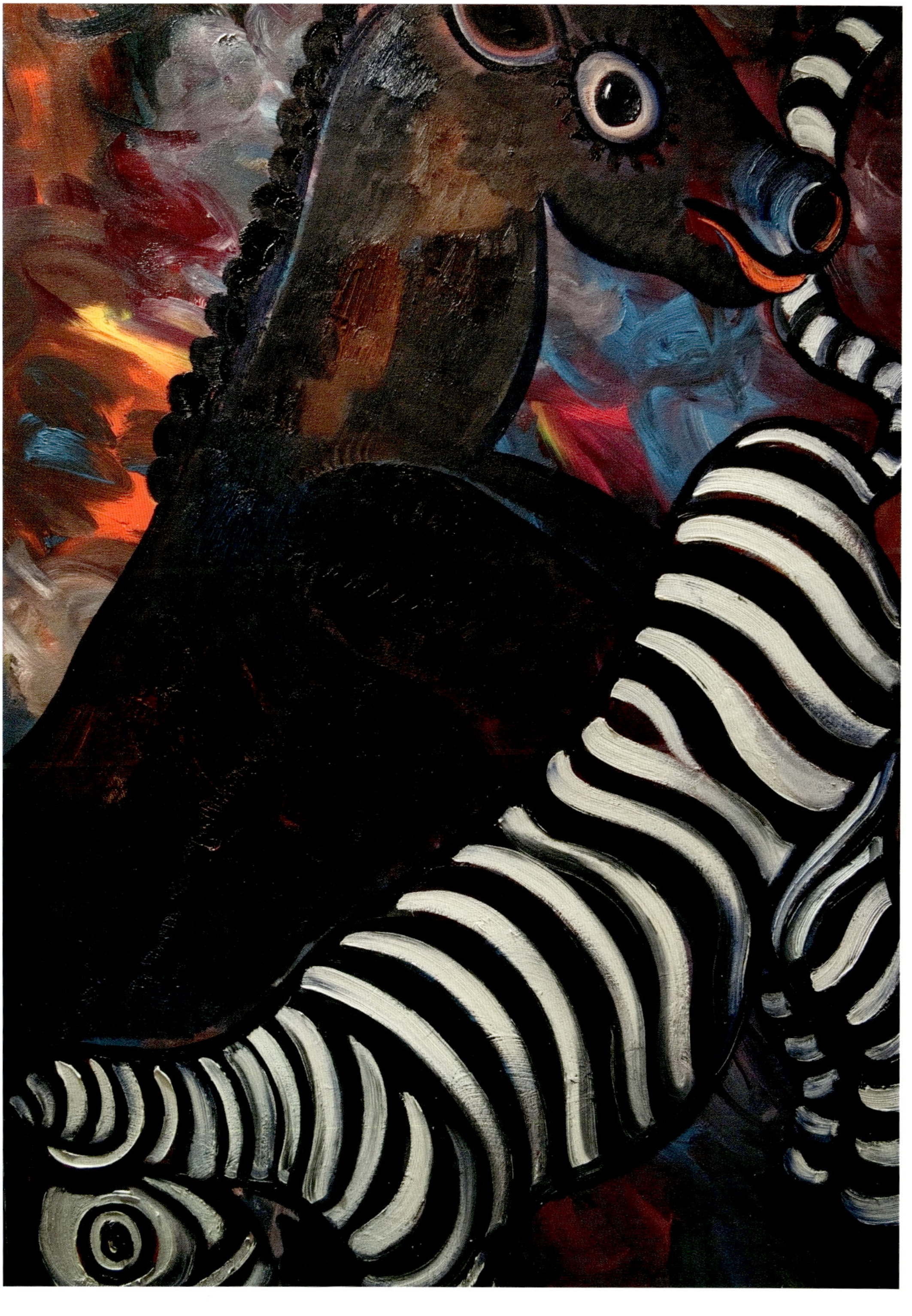

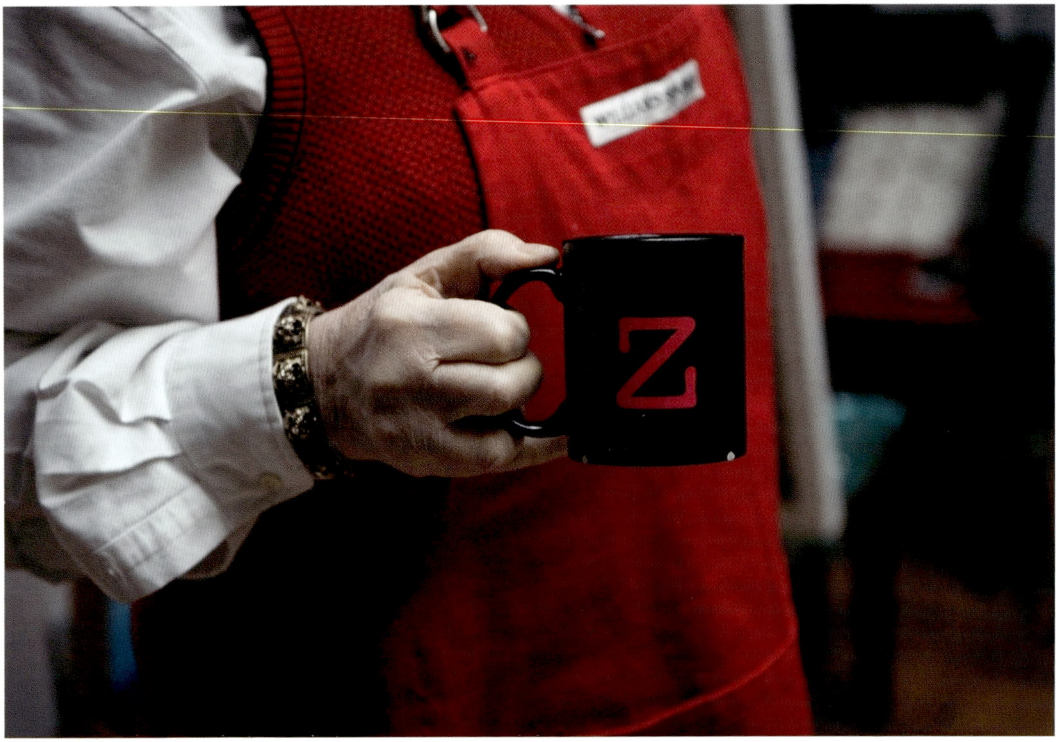

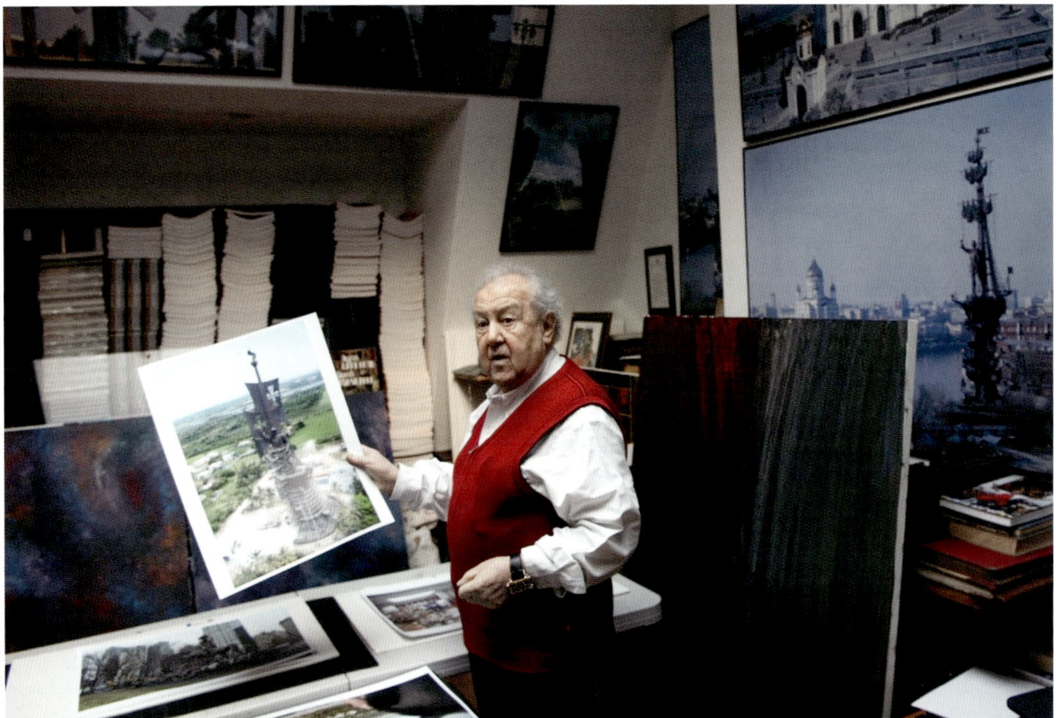

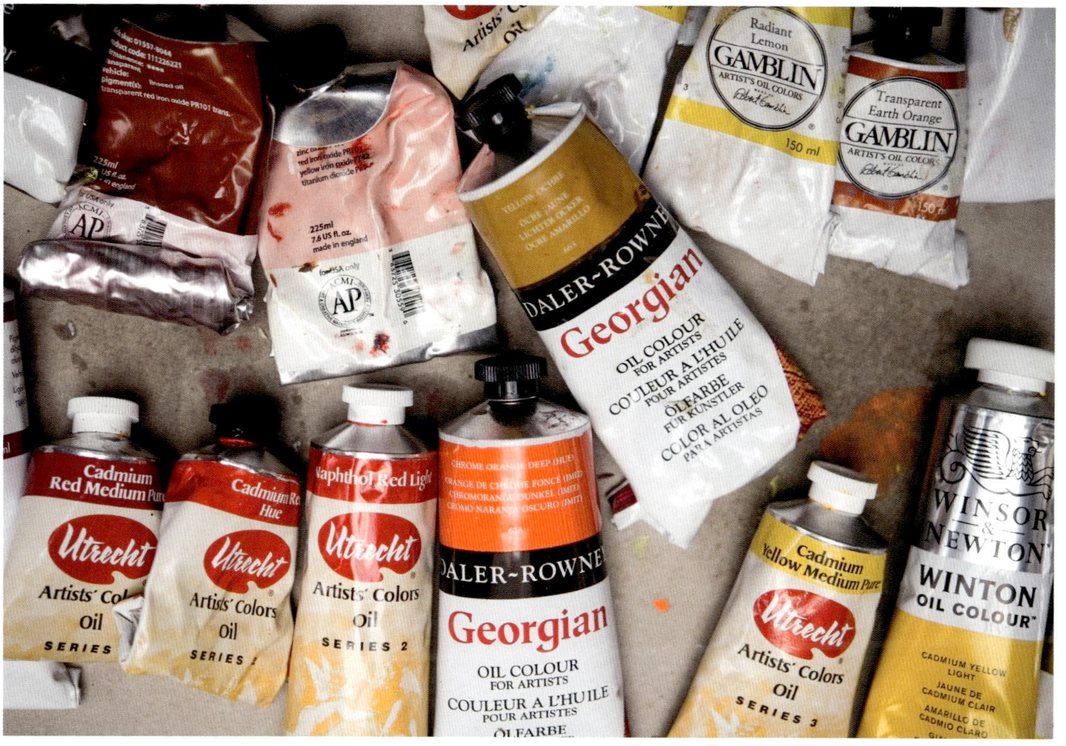
Radiant Lemon
GAMBLIN
ARTIST'S OIL COLORS
150 ml
Transparent Earth Orange
GAMBLIN
ARTIST'S OIL COLORS
225ml
7.6 US fl. oz.
made in england
DALER-ROWNEY
Georgian
OIL COLOUR
FOR ARTISTS
COULEUR A L'HUILE
POUR ARTISTES
ÖLFARBE
FÜR KÜNSTLER
COLOR AL OLEO
PARA ARTISTAS
Cadmium Red Medium Pure
Utrecht
Artists' Colors
Oil
SERIES
Cadmium Red Hue
Utrecht
Artists' Colors
Oil
Naphthol Red Light
Utrecht
Artists' Colors
Oil
SERIES 2
CHROME ORANGE DEEP (HUE)
DALER-ROWNEY
Georgian
OIL COLOUR
FOR ARTISTS
COULEUR A L'HUILE
POUR ARTISTES
Cadmium Yellow Medium Pure
Utrecht
Artists' Colors
Oil
SERIES 3
WINSOR & NEWTON
WINTON
OIL COLOUR
CADMIUM YELLOW LIGHT
JAUNE DE CADMIUM CLAIR
AMARILLO DE CADMIO CLARO

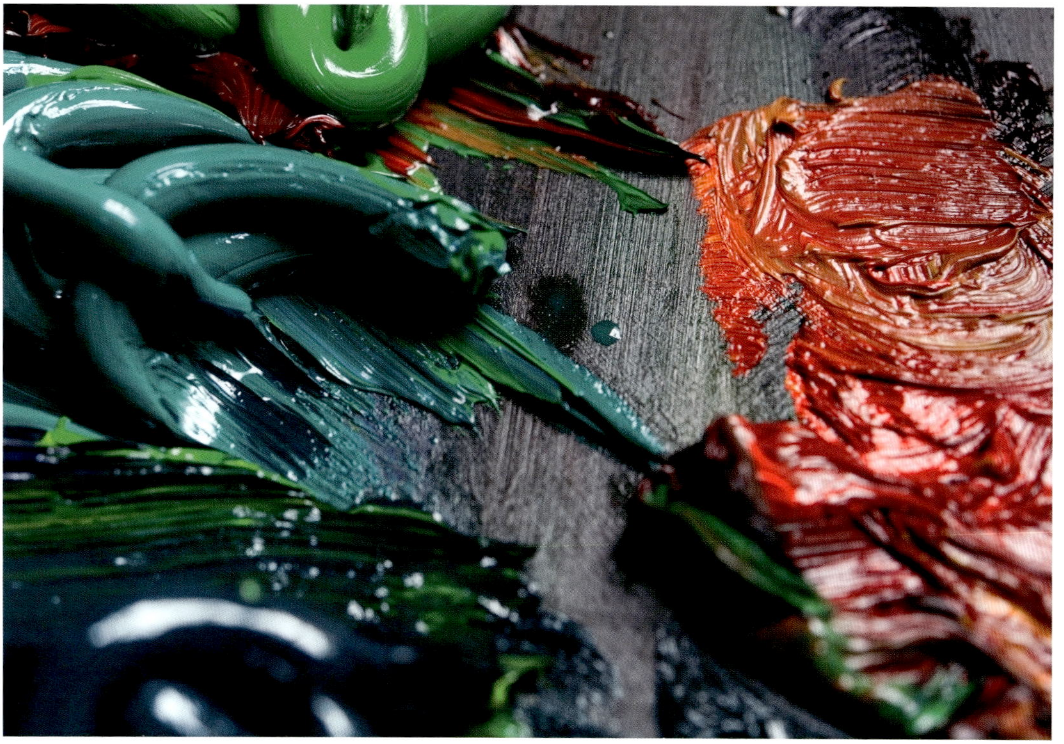

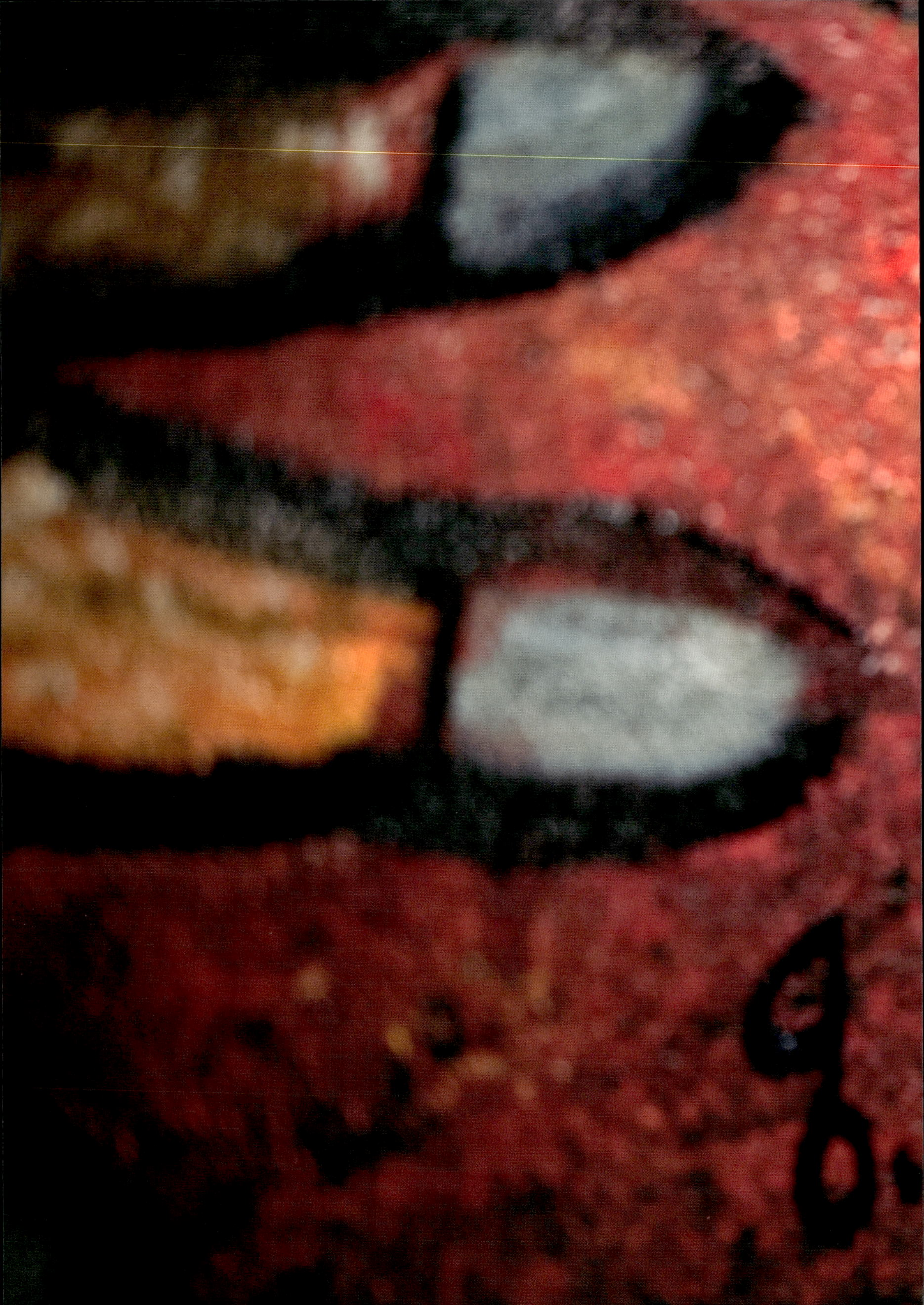

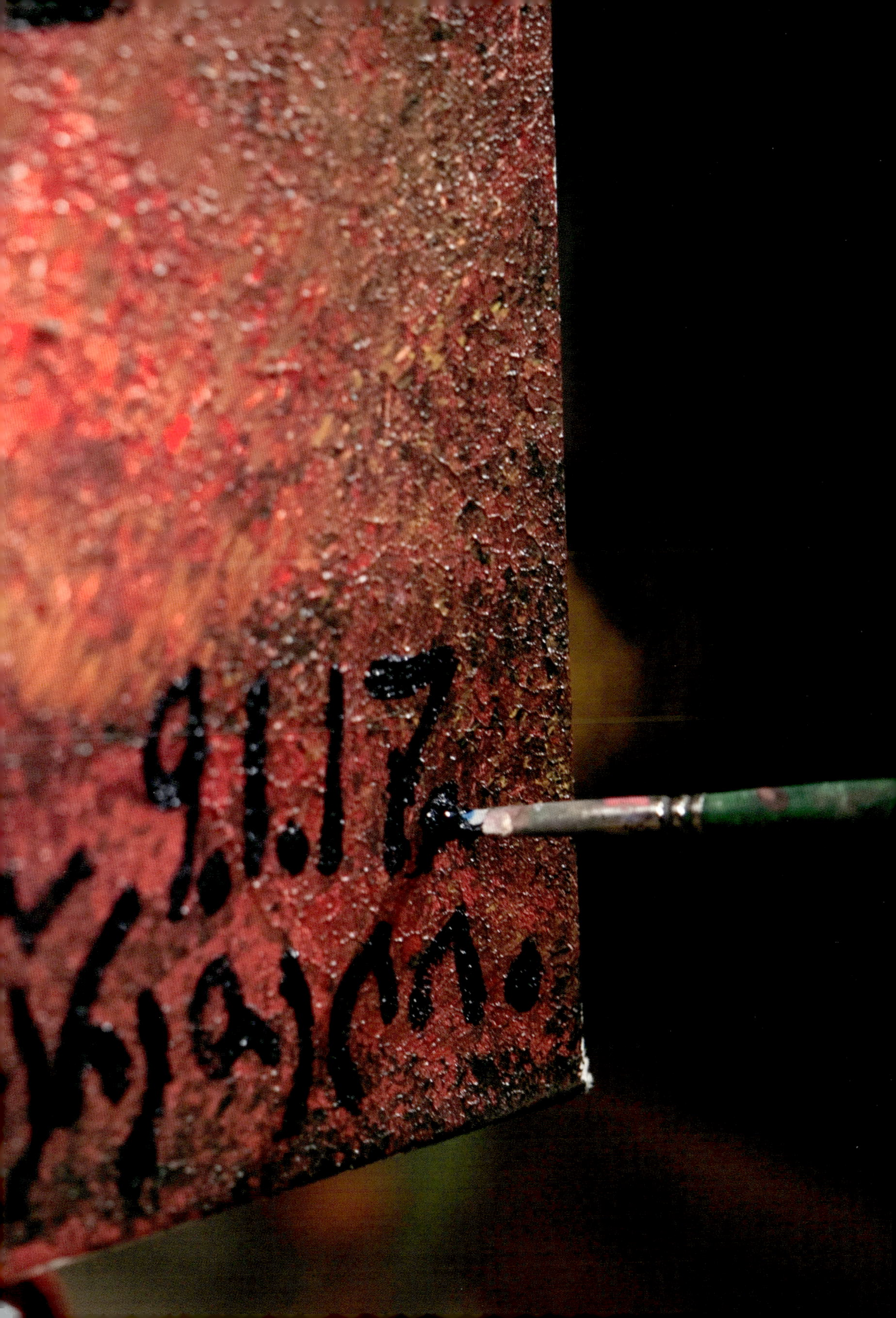

Paris

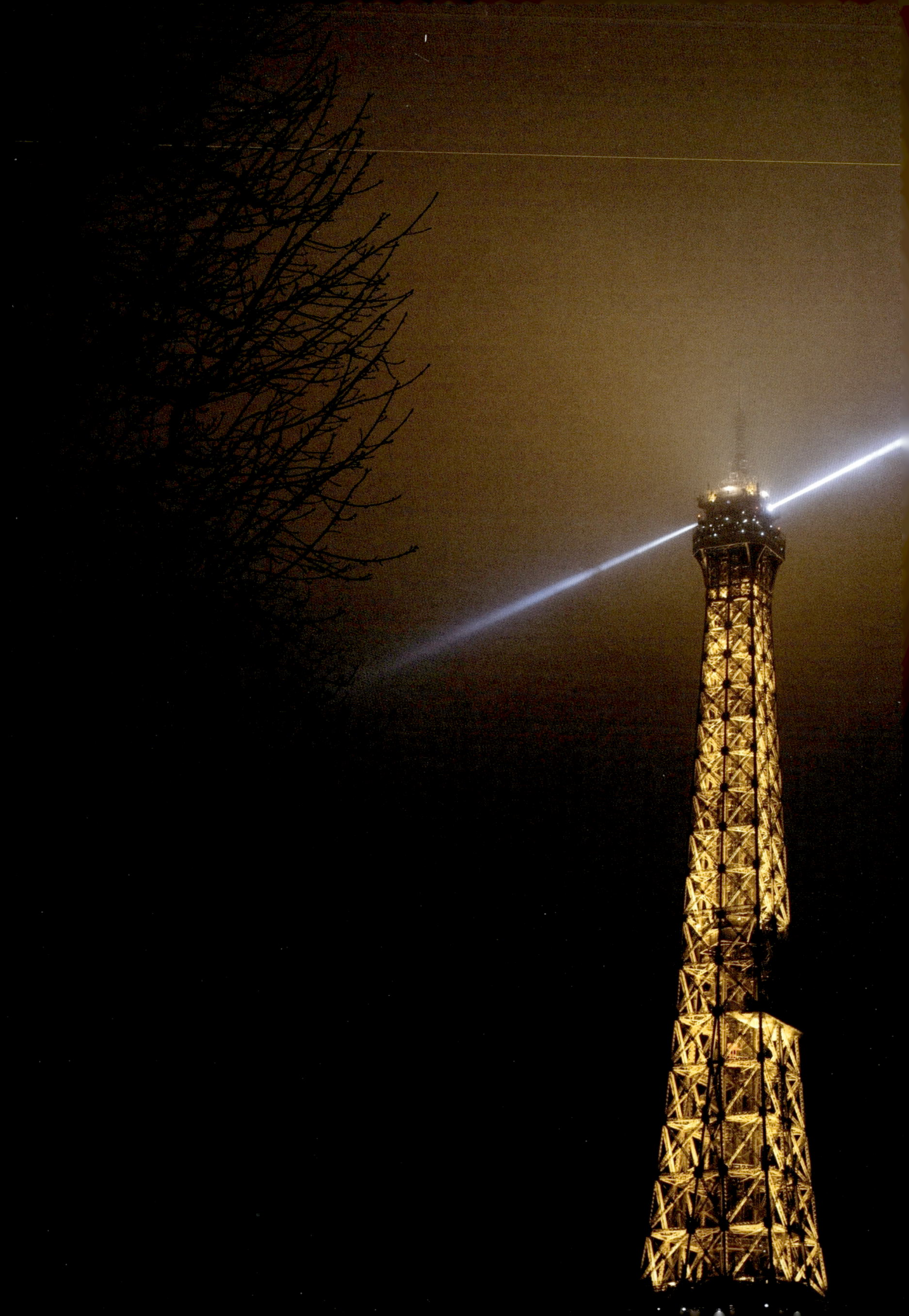

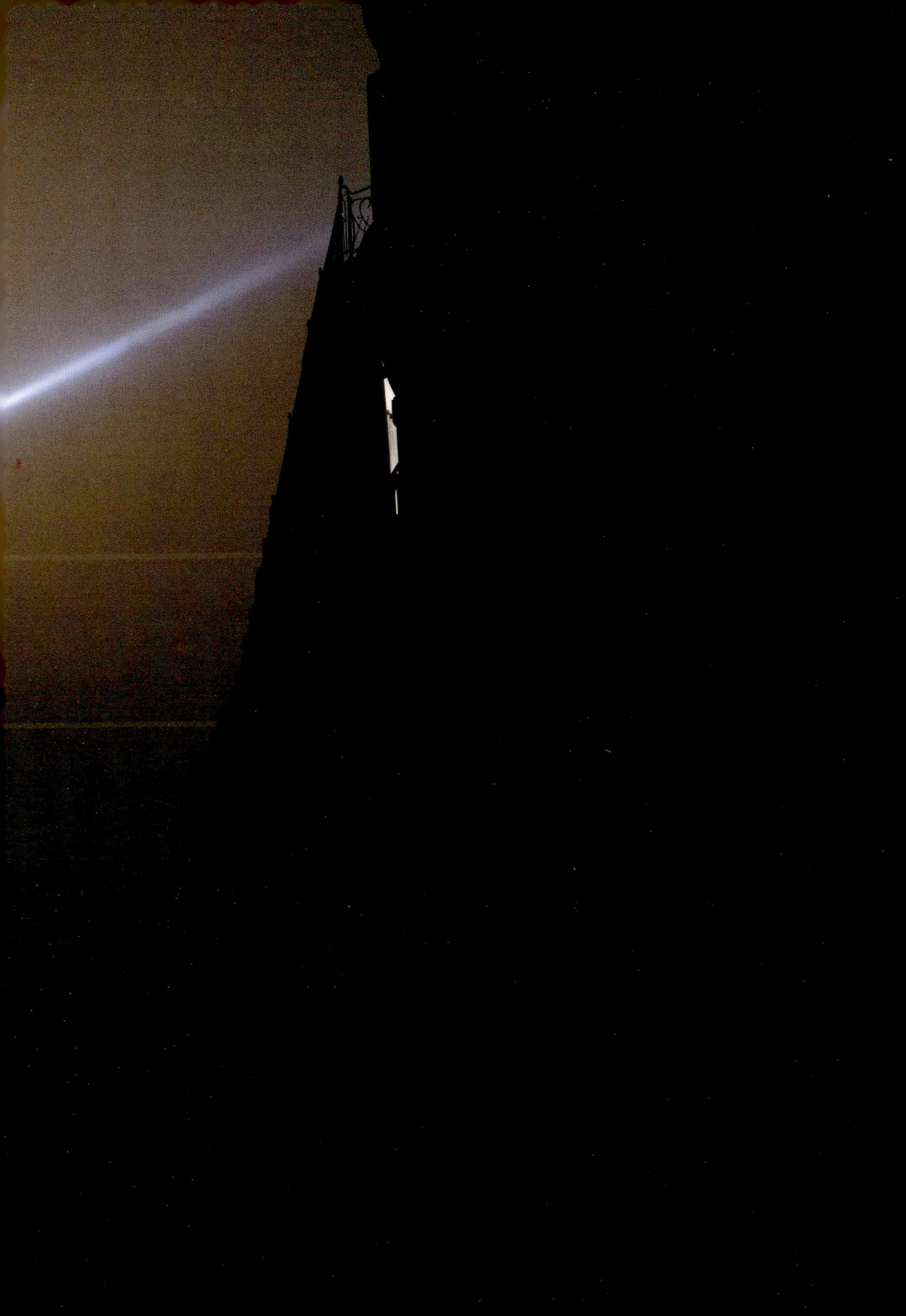

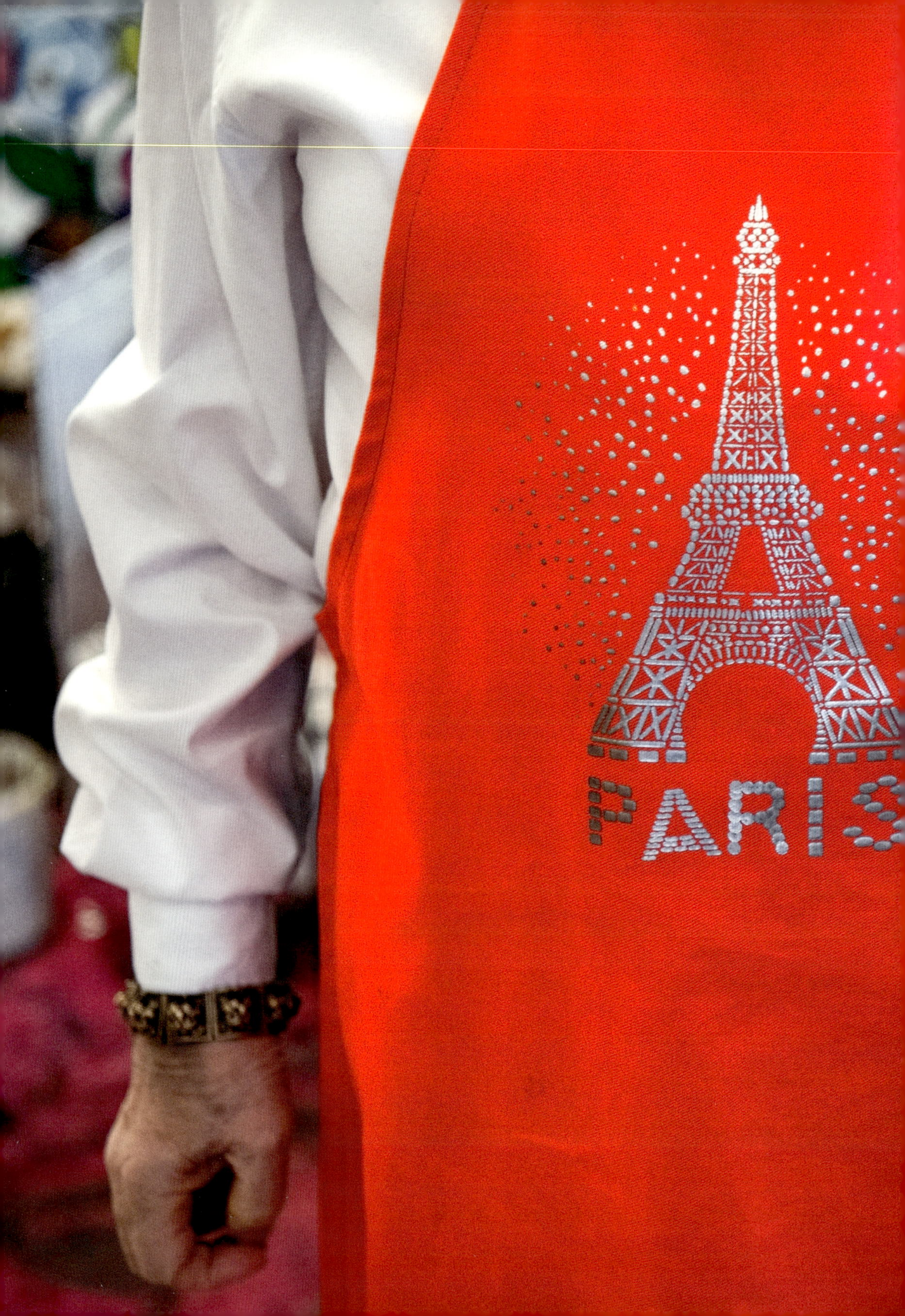
PARIS

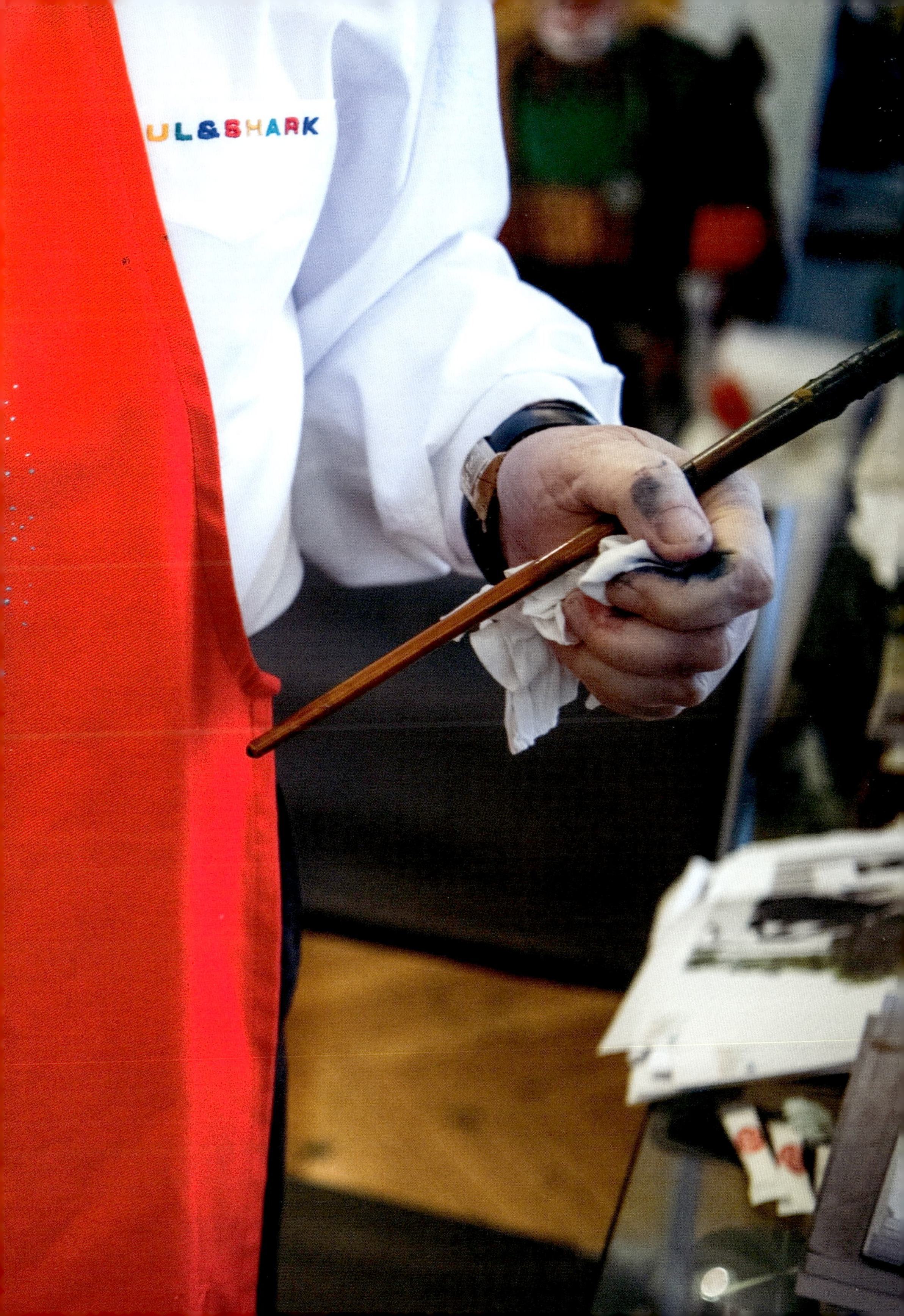
UL&SHARK

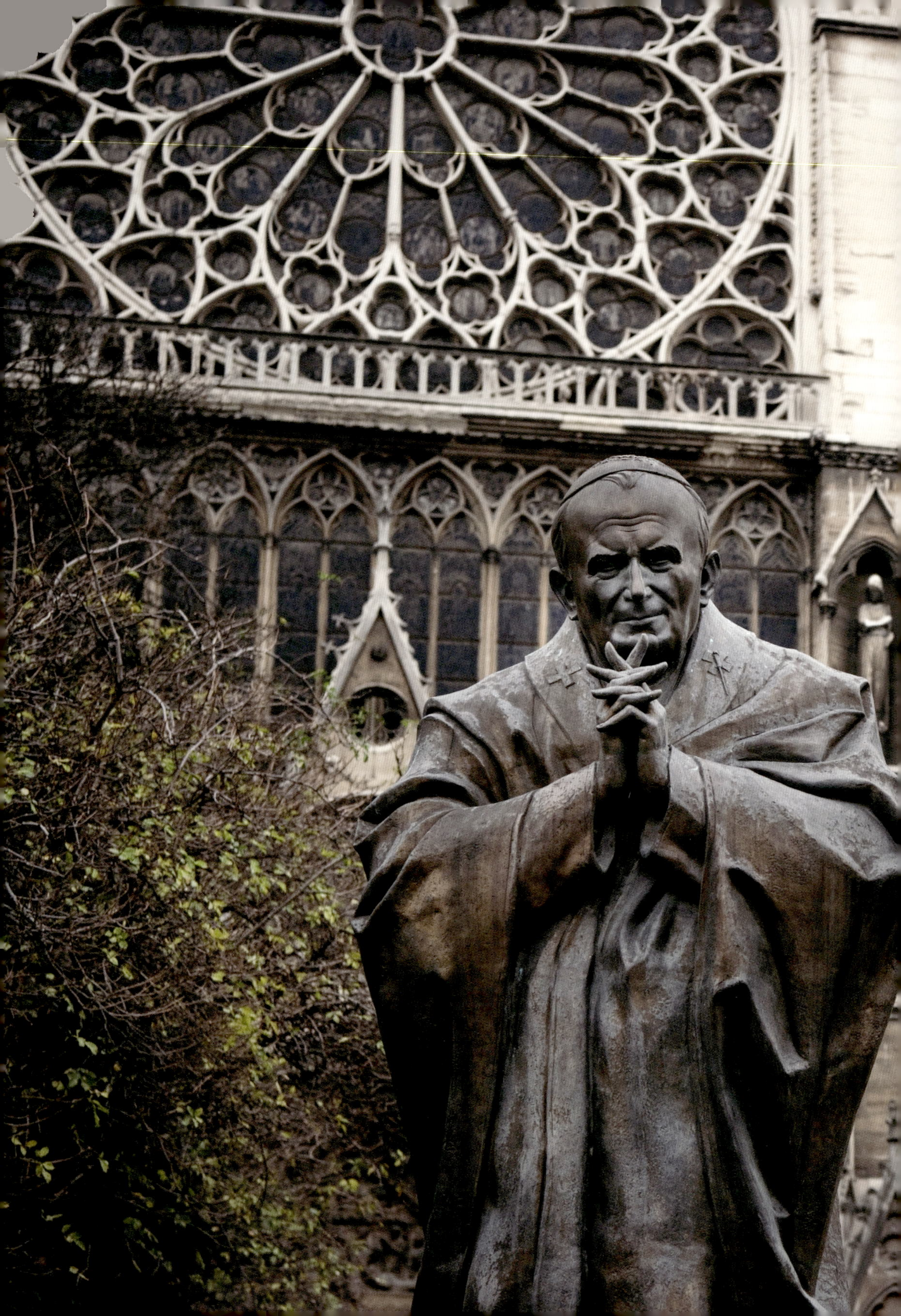

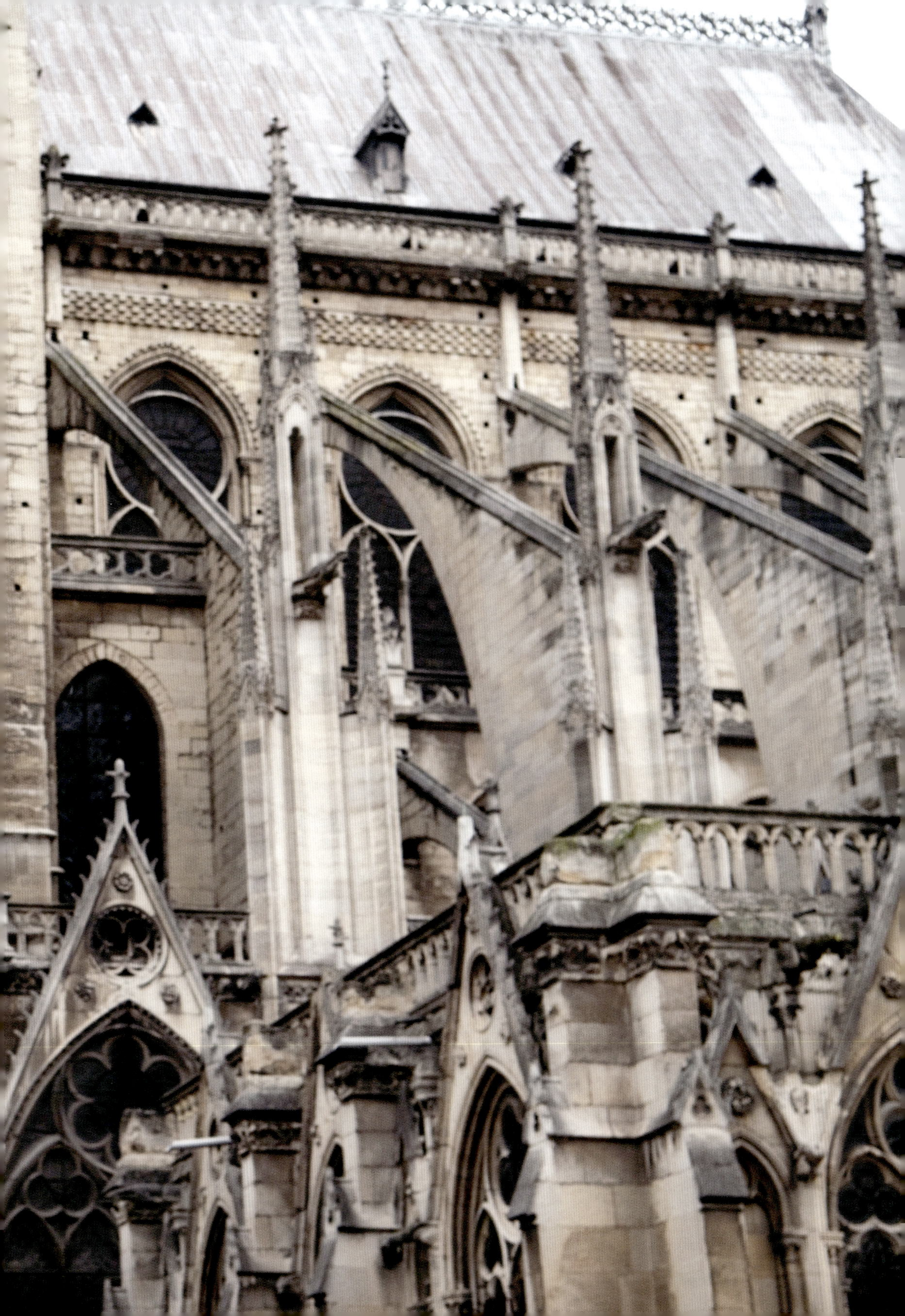

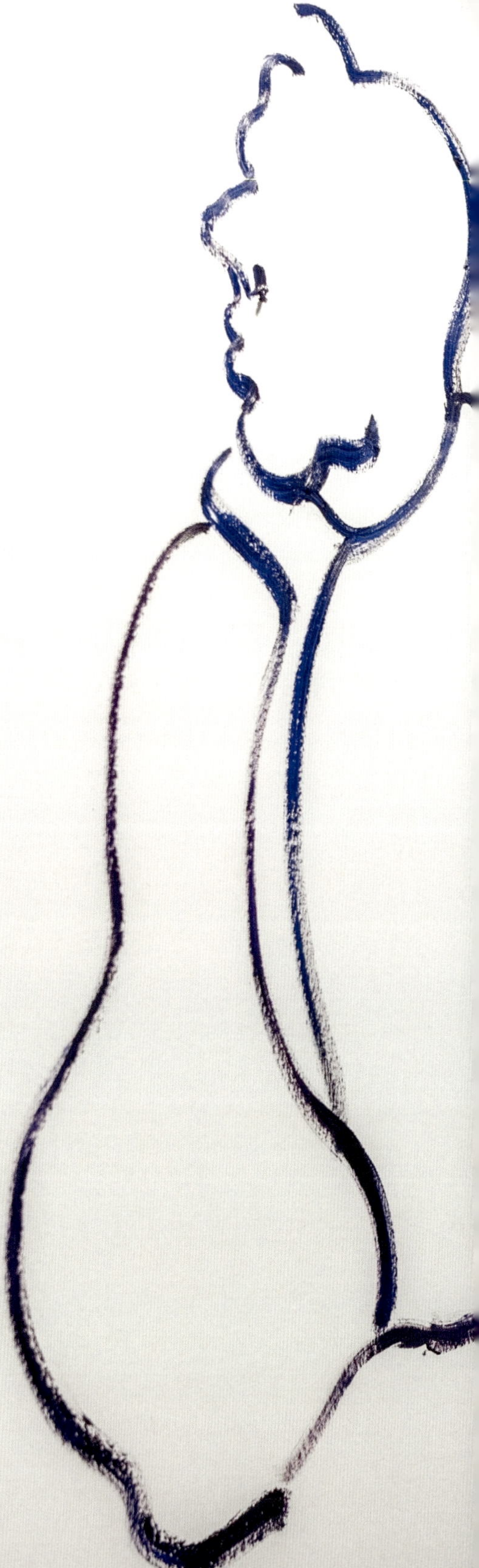

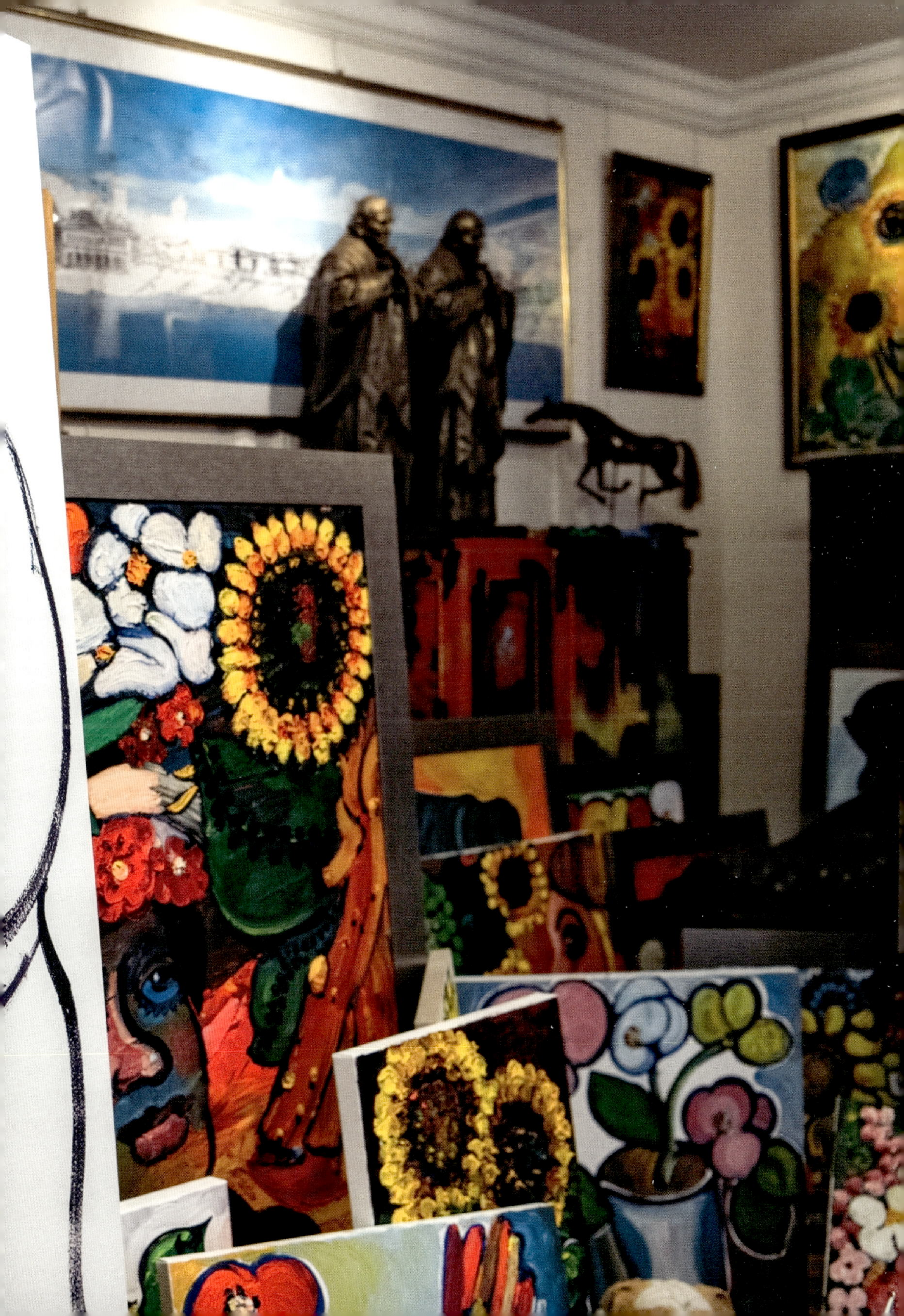

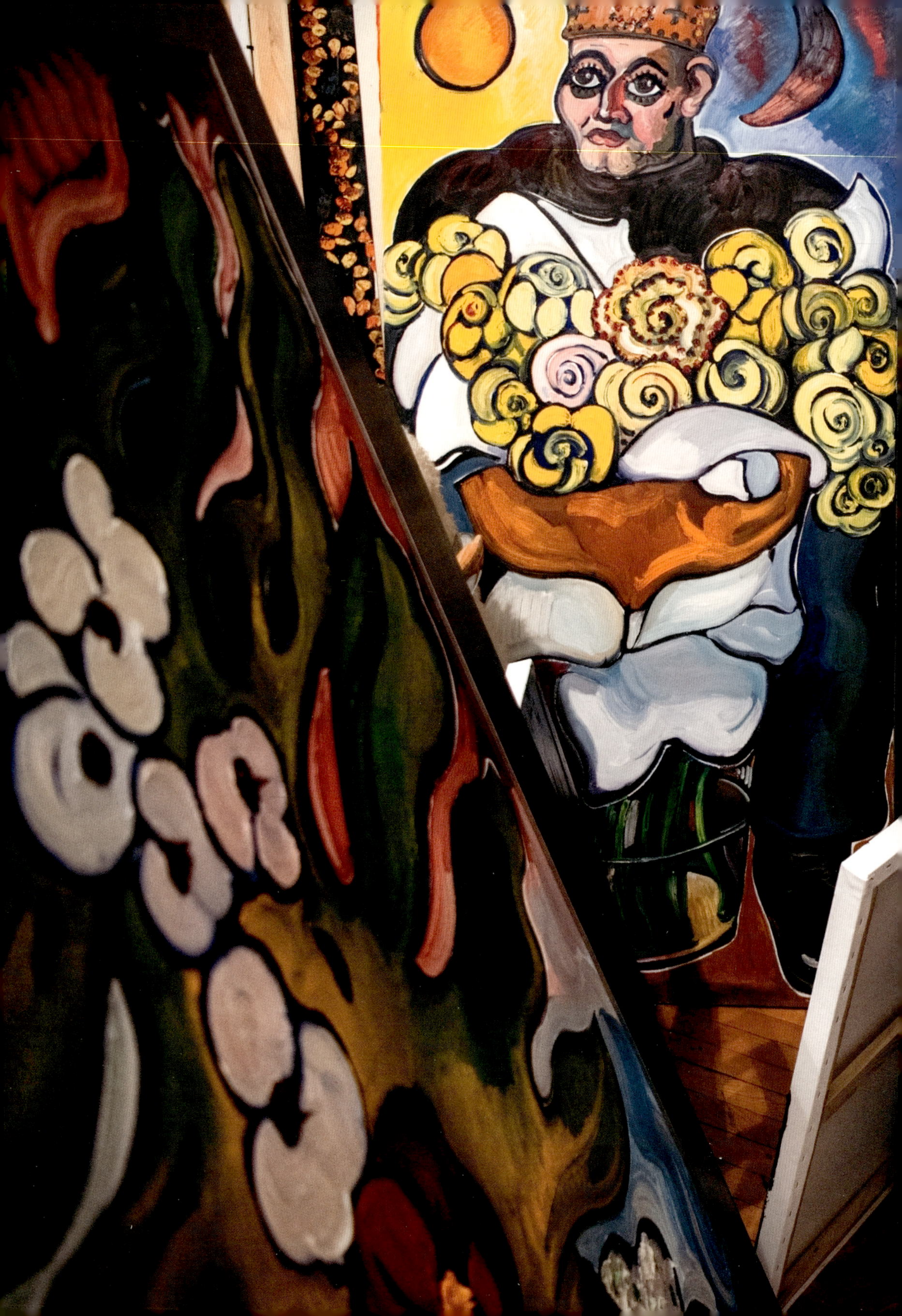

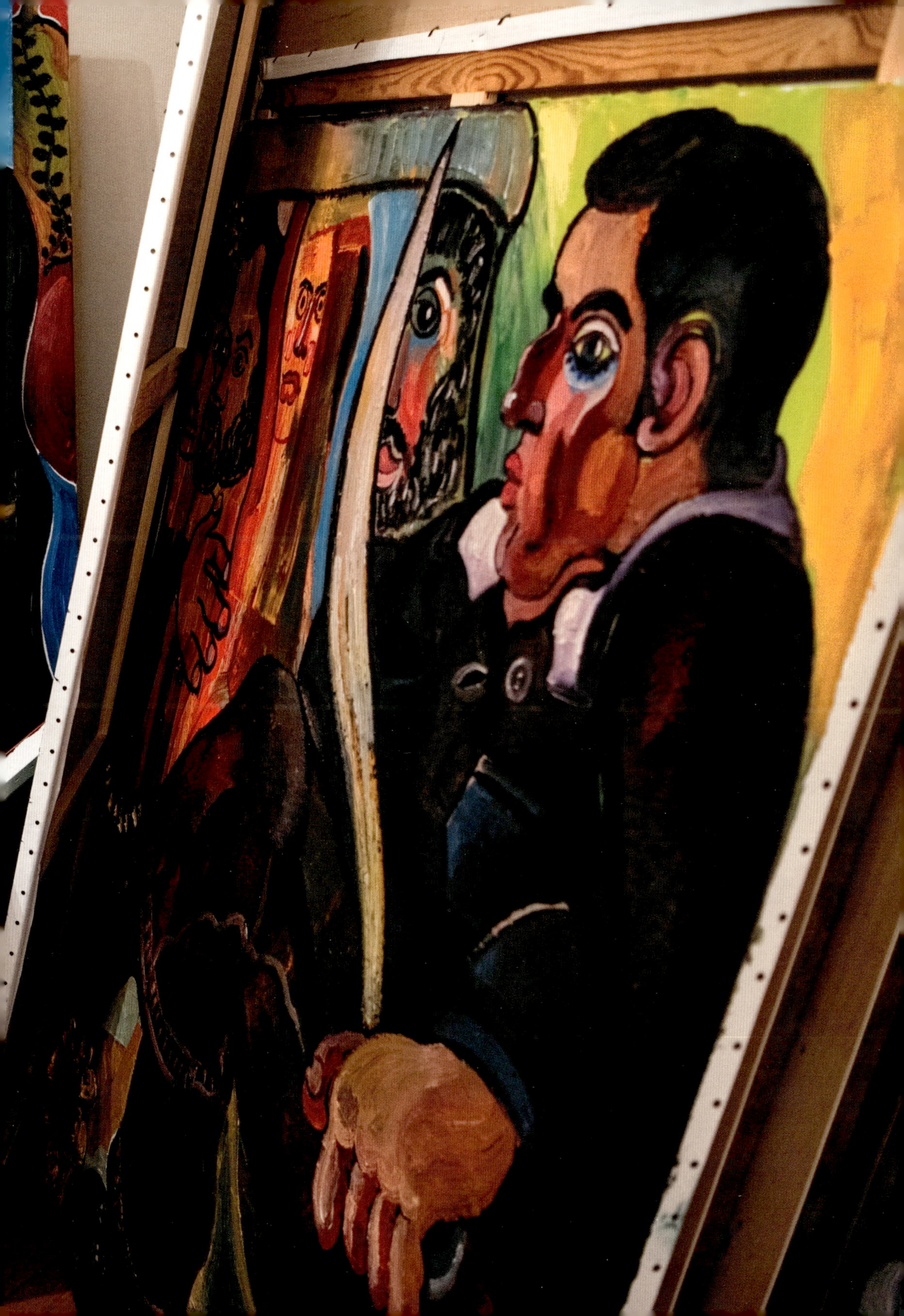

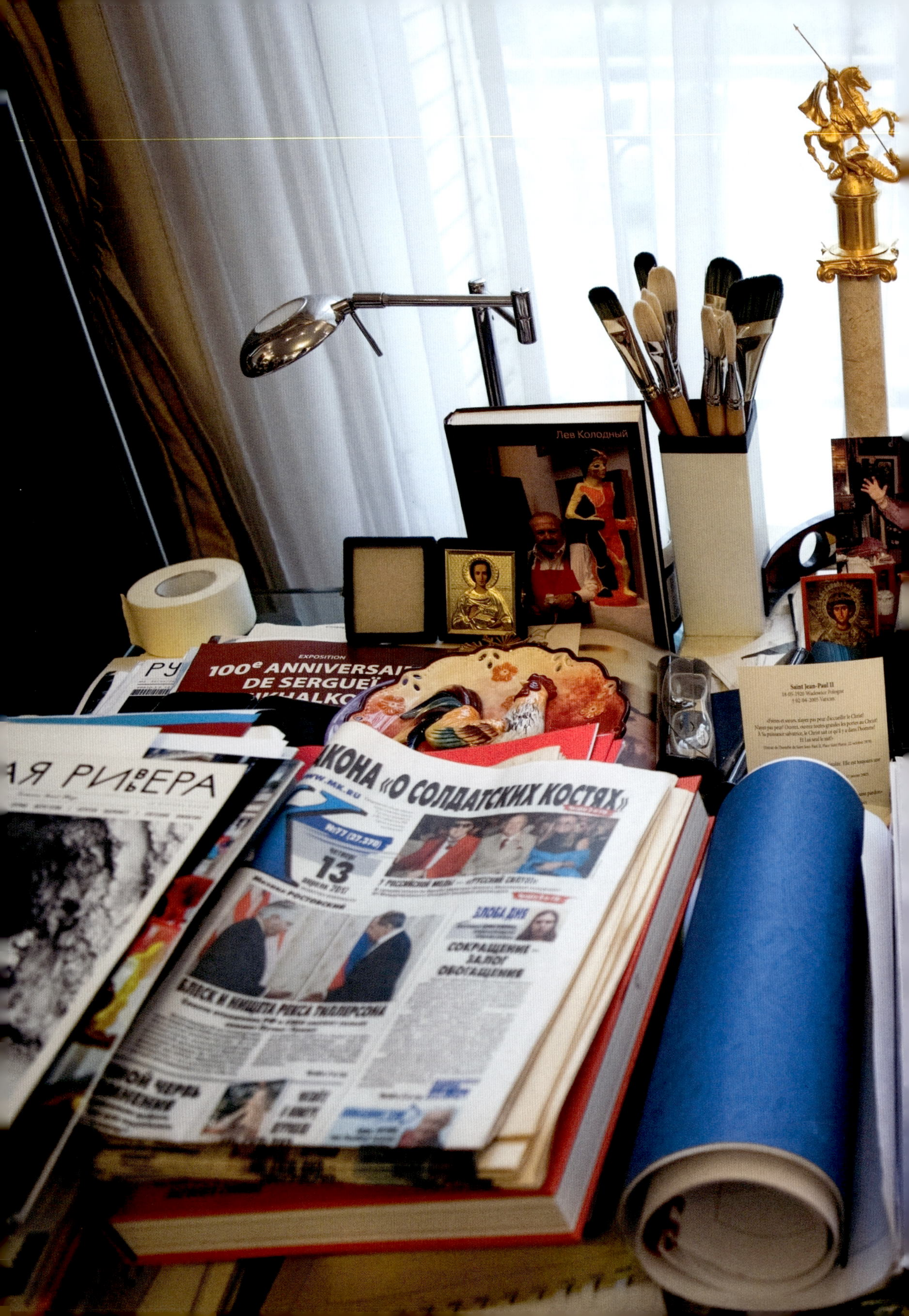
Лев Колодный
EXPOSITION
«О СОЛДАТСКИХ КОСТЯХ»
www.mk.ru
13
ЗЛОБА ДНЯ
СОКРАЩЕНИЕ – ЗАЛОГ ОБОГАЩЕНИЯ
БЛЕСК И НИЩЕТА РЕКСА ТИЛЛЕРСОНА
Saint Jean-Paul II

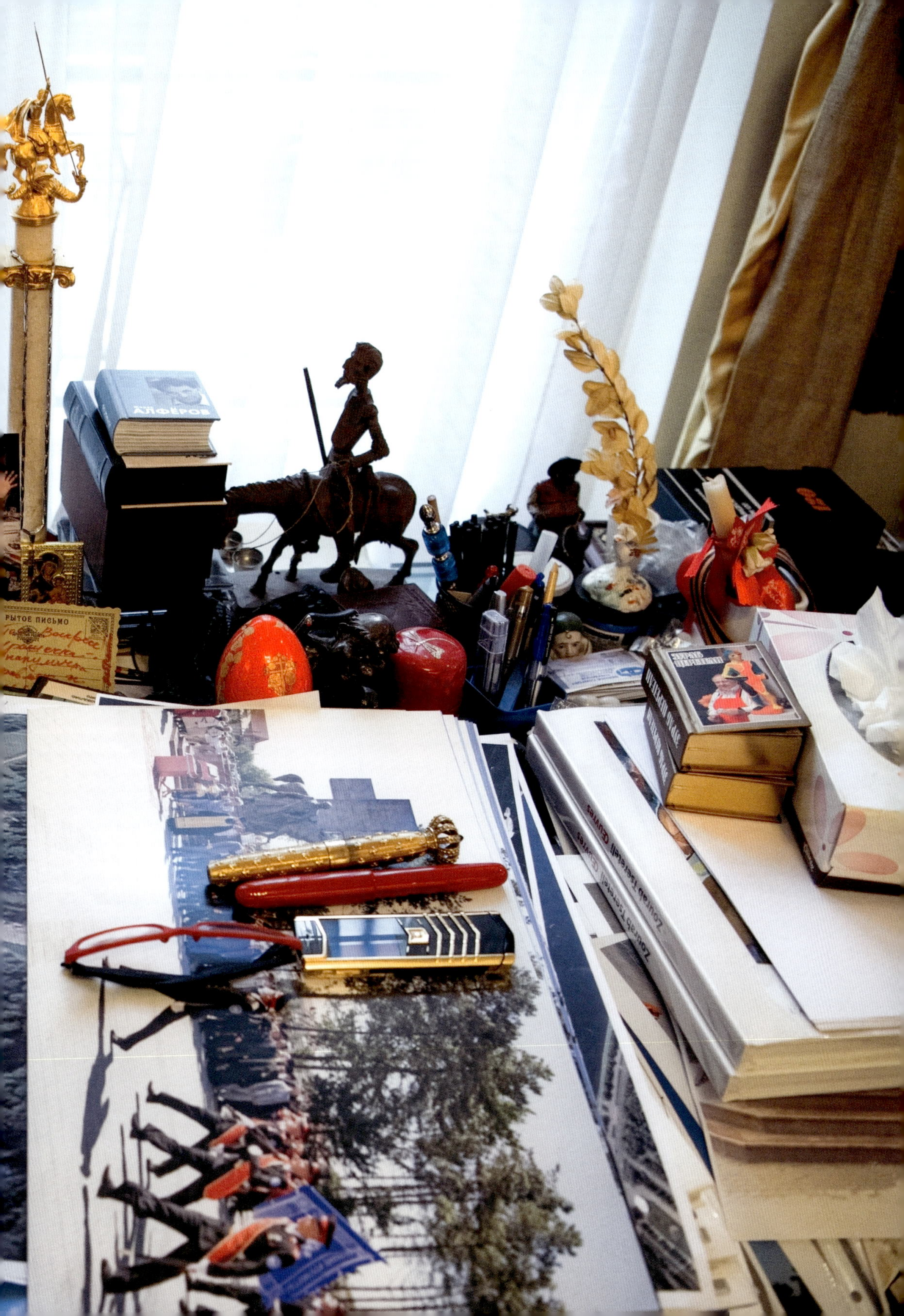
АЛФЁРОВ
РЫТОЕ ПИСЬМО
Zourab Tsereteli Œuvres
Zourab Tsereteli Œuvres

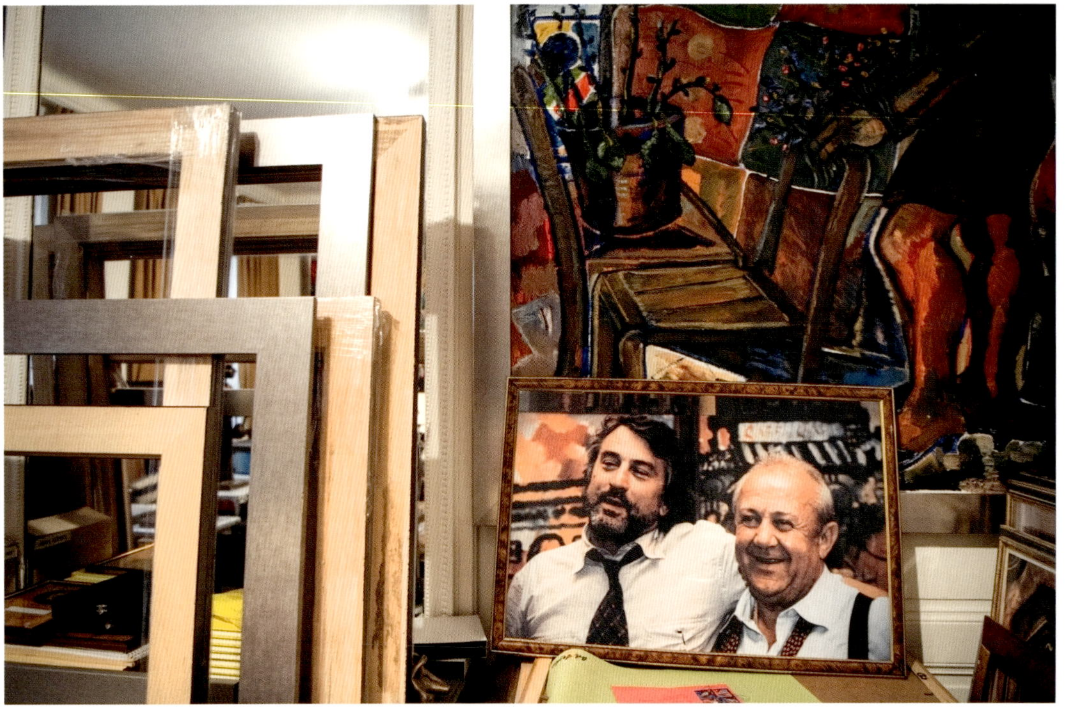

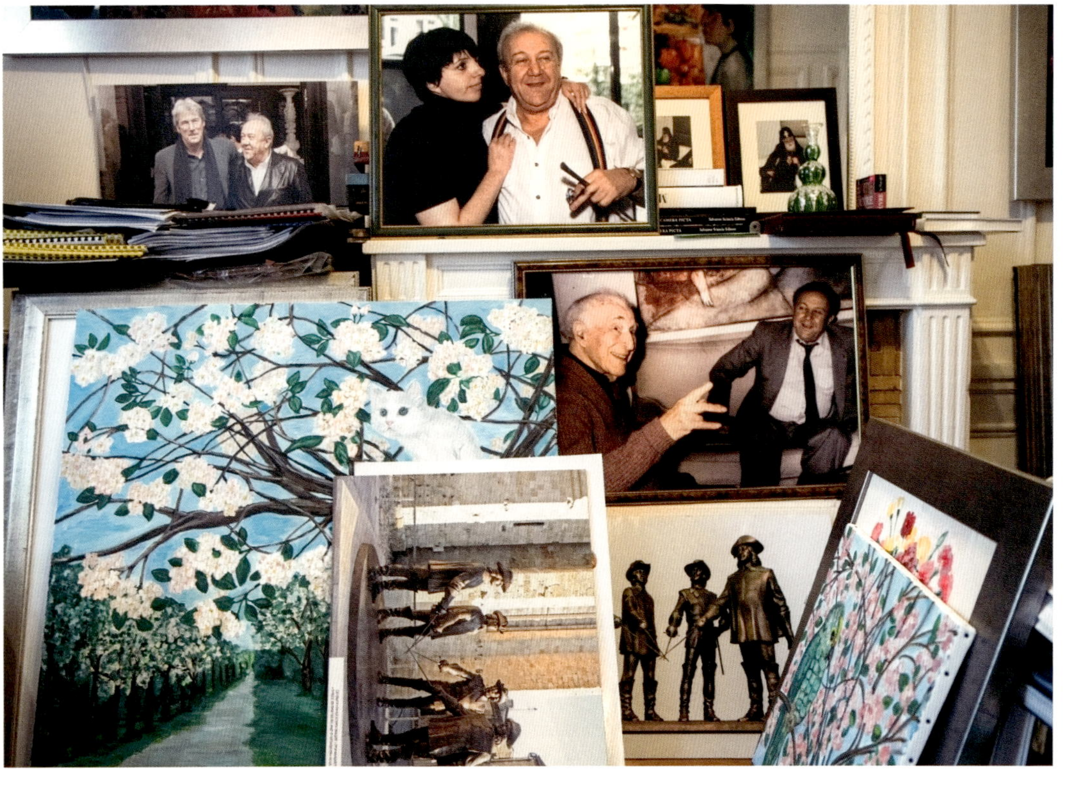

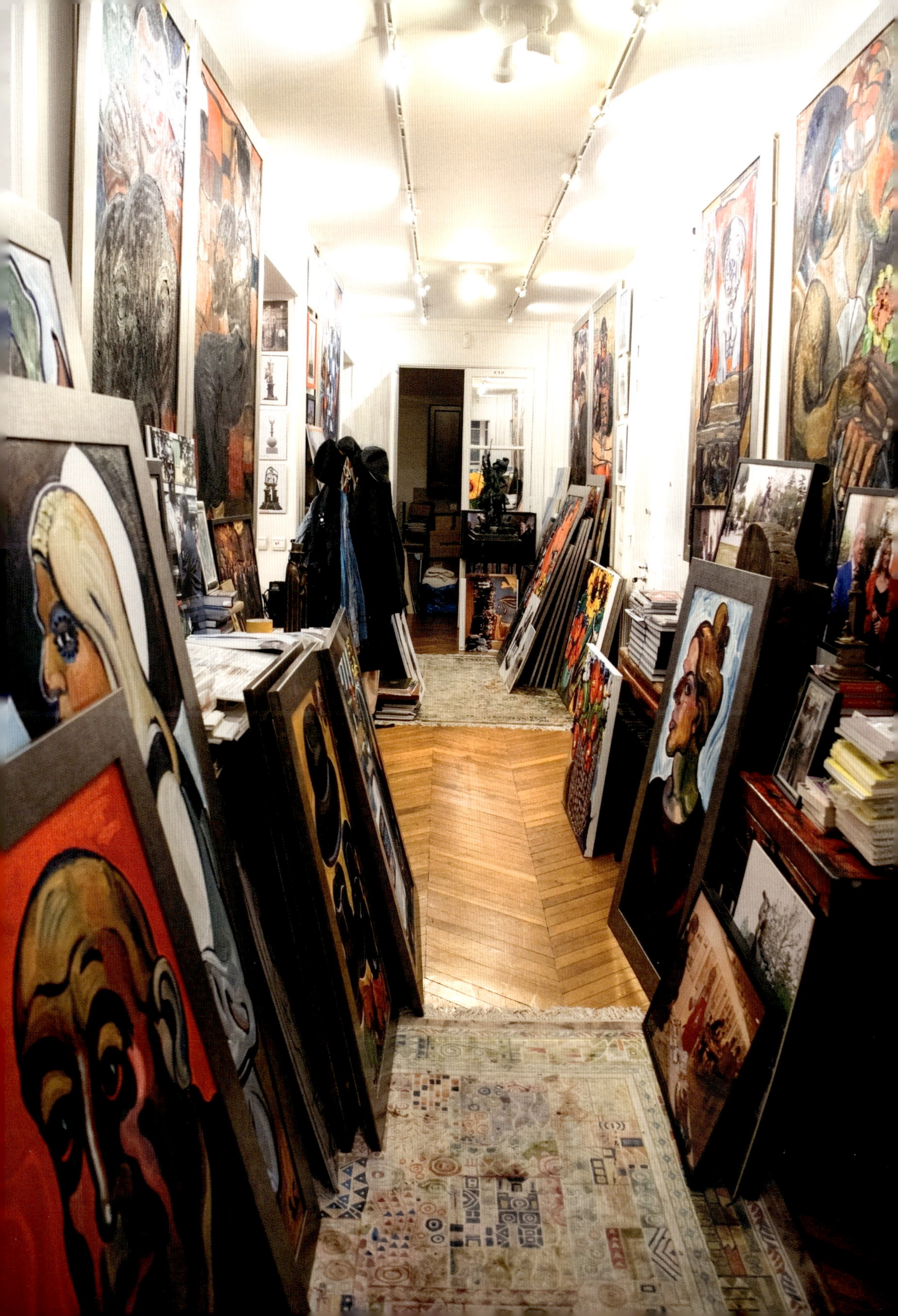

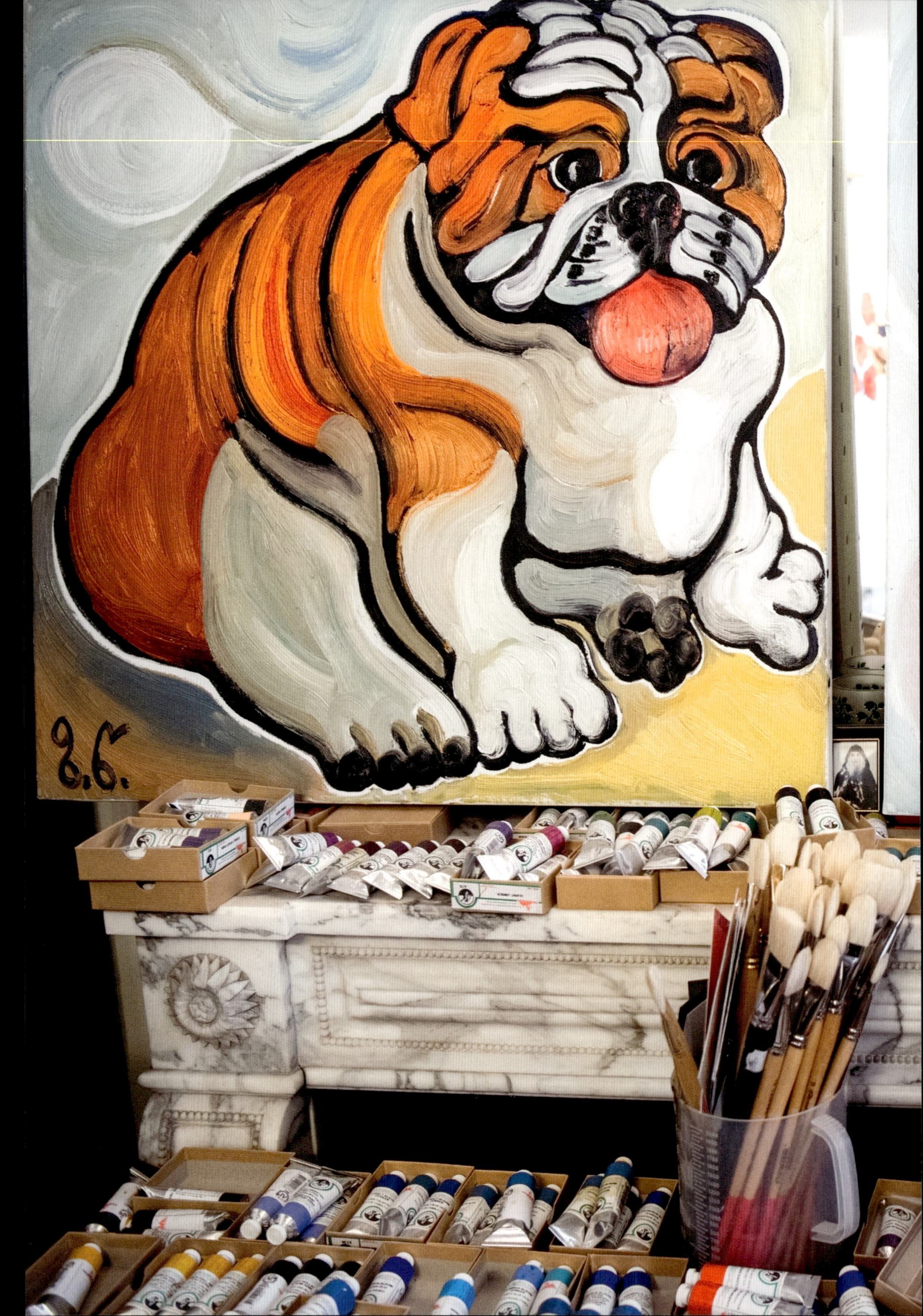

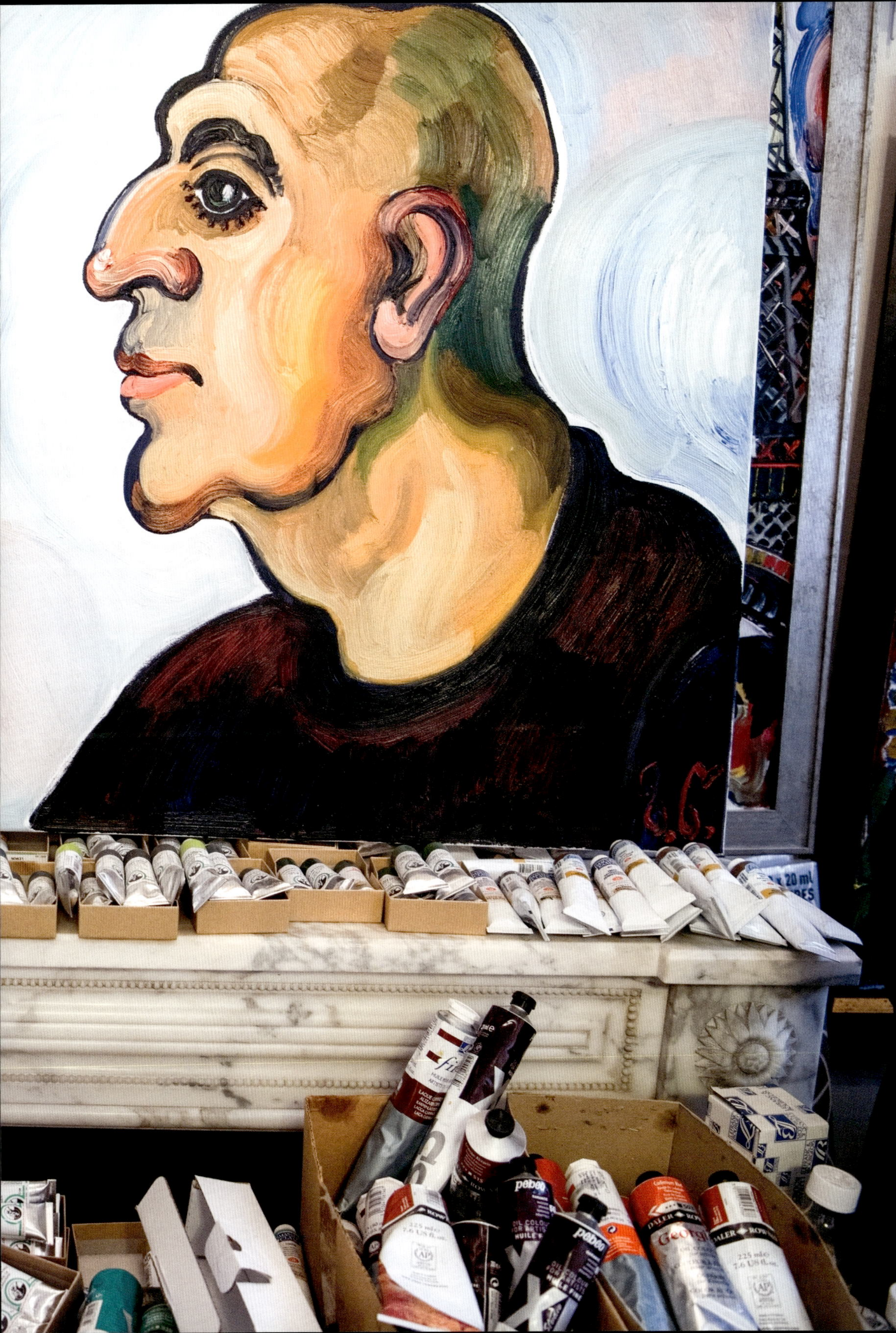
pebeo
pebeo
DALER-ROWNEY
DALER-ROWNEY

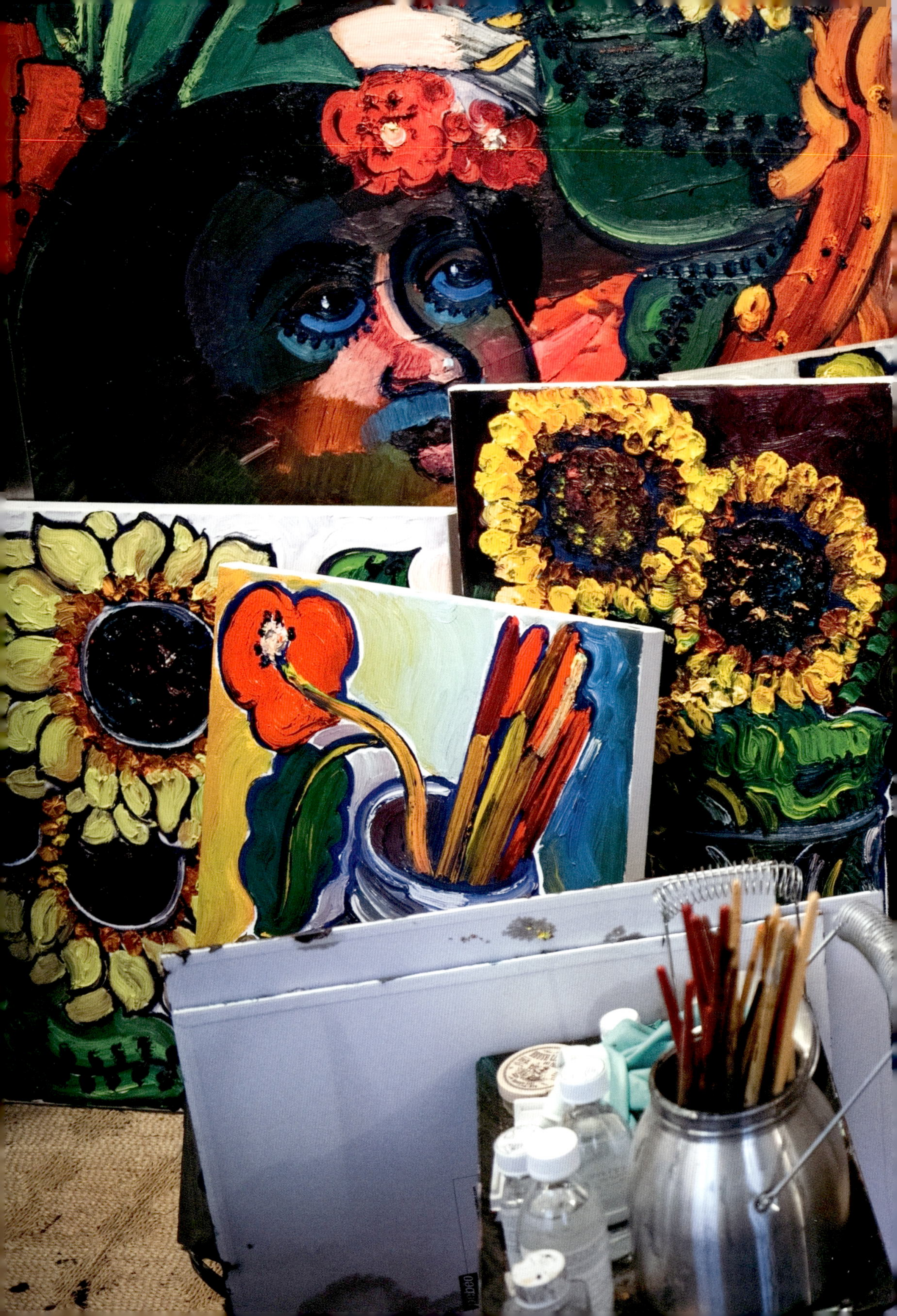

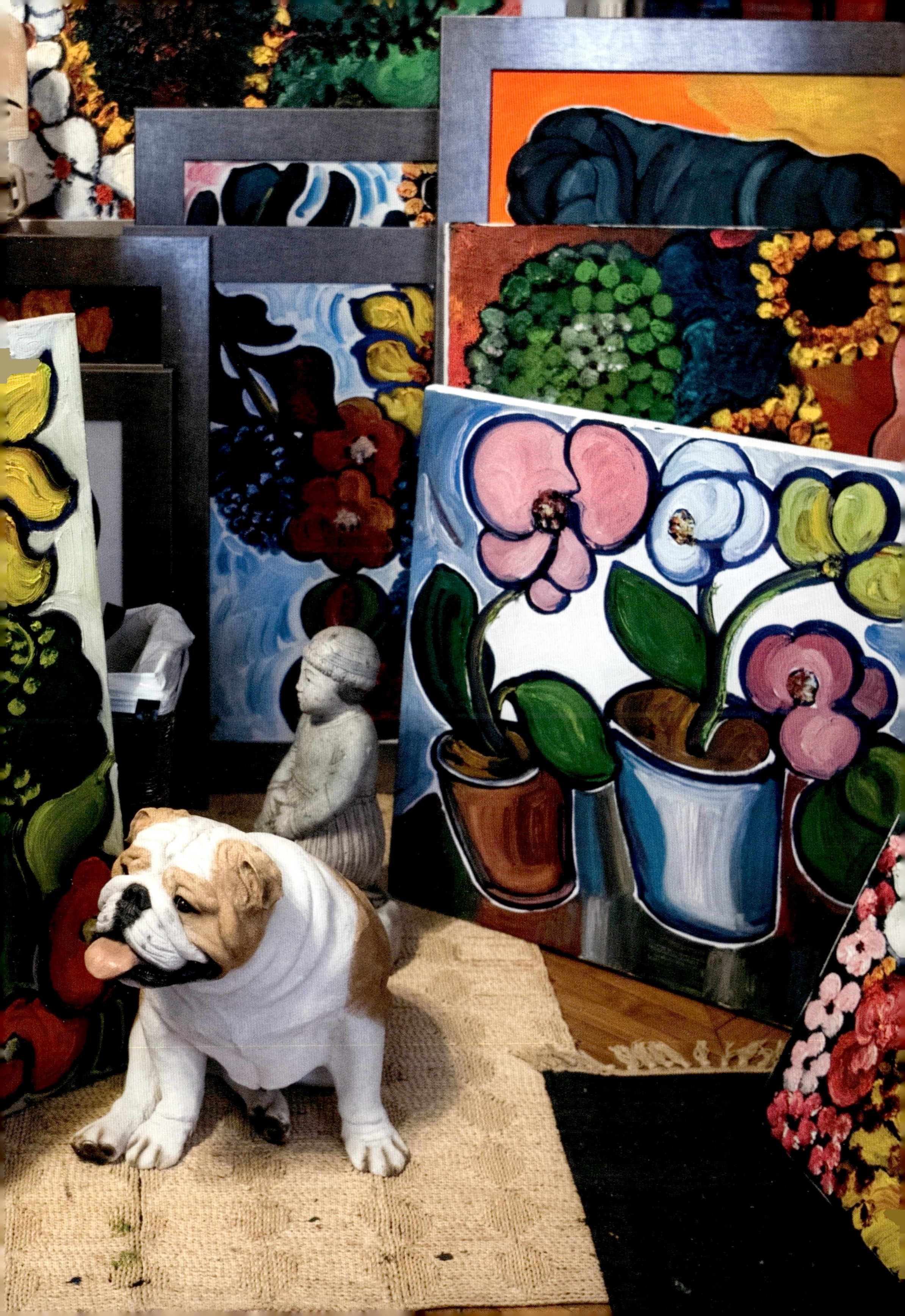

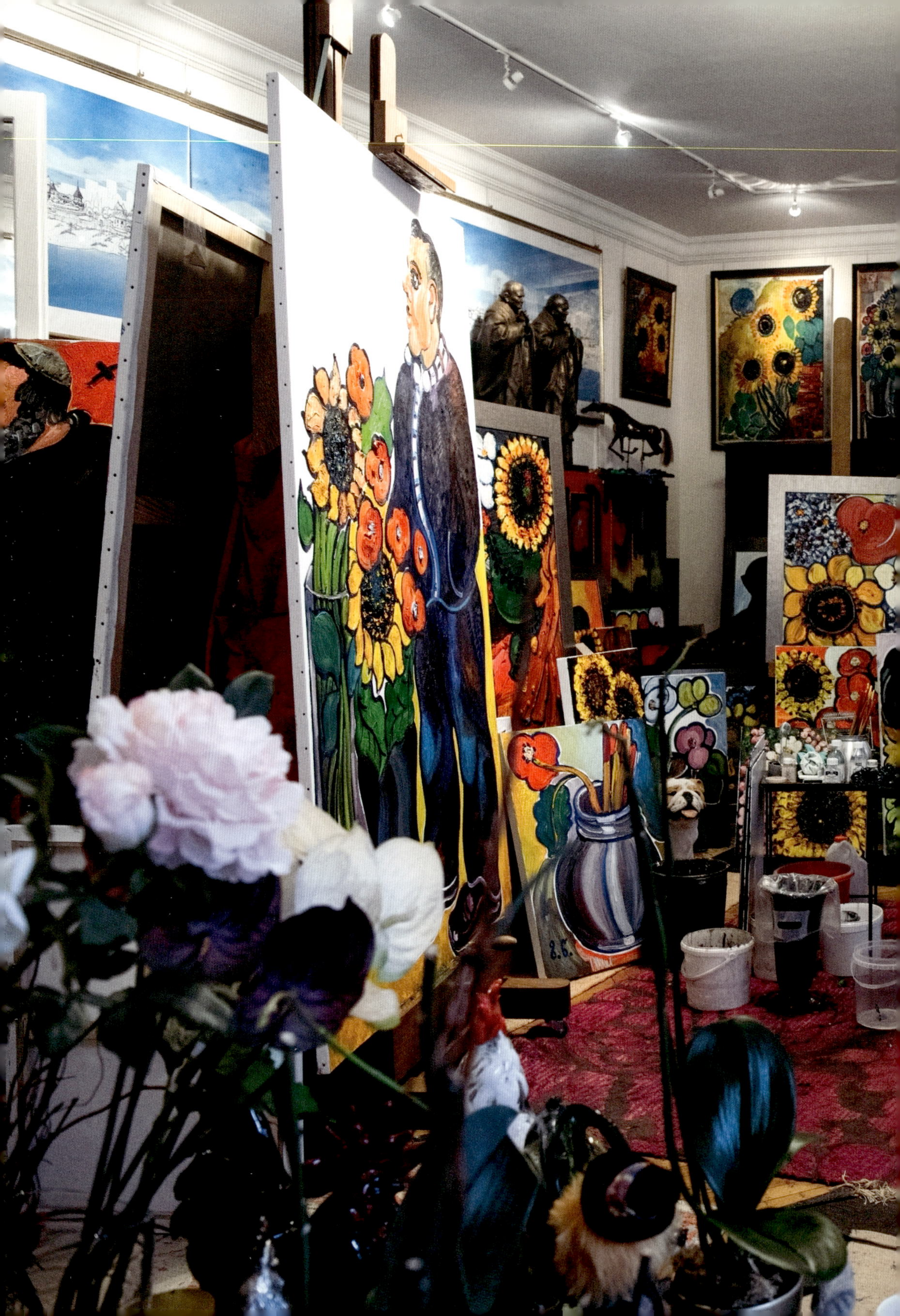

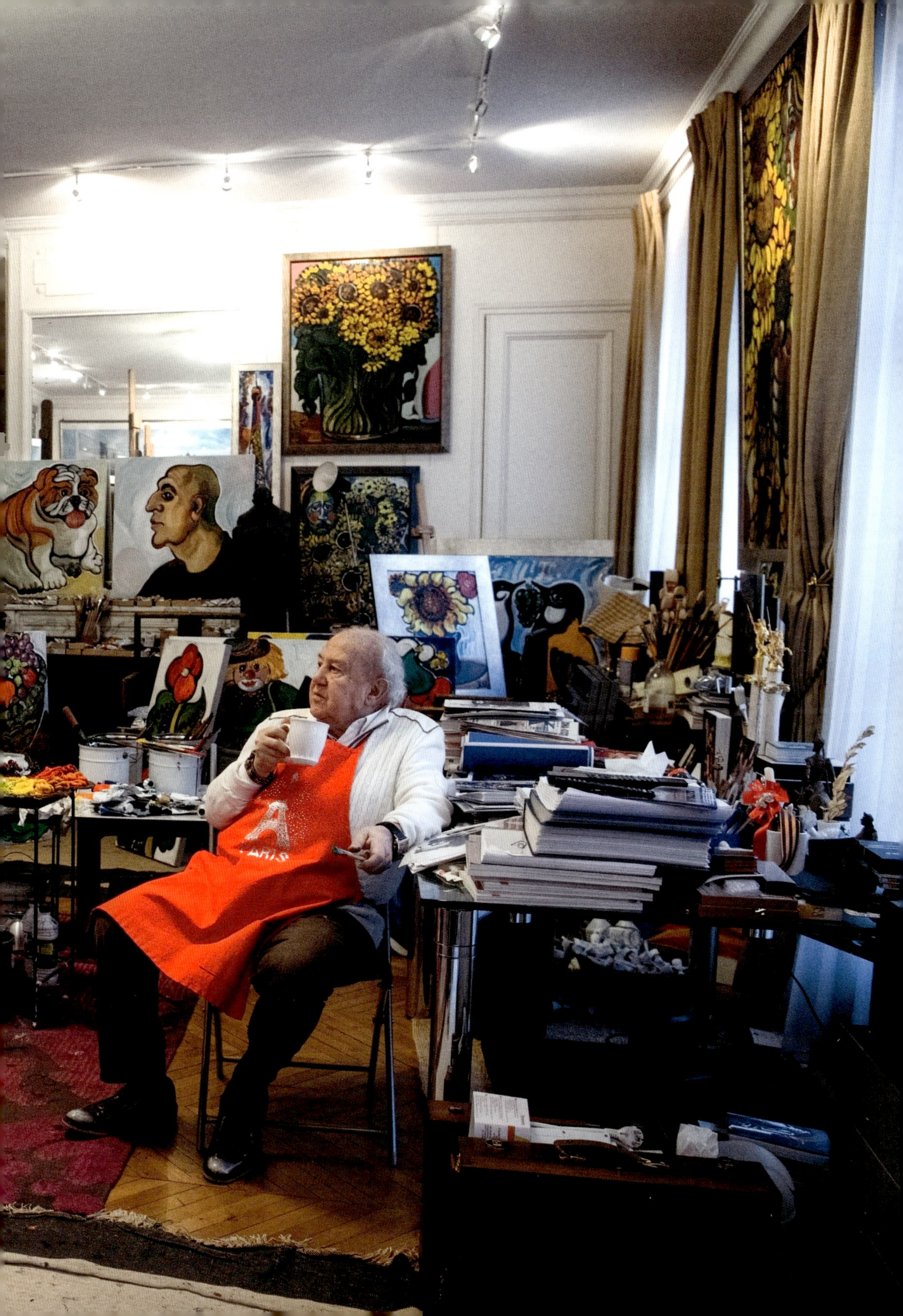

Biographies

Zurab Konstantinovich Tsereteli was born in Tbilisi on January 4, 1934. As a child he took a great interest in drawing and painting, encouraged by his uncle, the artist Giorgi Nijaradze. Following this passion, after school he enrolled in the Painting Department of the Tbilisi State Academy of Arts in 1952, graduating in 1958, the year of his marriage to Inessa Andronikashvili.

In 1960–1963, Tsereteli worked as a staff artist at the Institute of History, Ethnography, and Archaeology of the Georgian Academy of Sciences, travelling all over the republic as part of research expeditions, discovering its ancient monuments, its folk-art tradition, and its rich material culture. Expanding the range of his creative possibilities, Tsereteli then took a position as a senior master at the industrial combine of the USSR's Arts Foundation in Tbilisi. There, he began experimenting with such media as bronze, stone, glass, wood, and mosaics, working on group commissions for public buildings—in a few years, he became the head of a production facility of this institution.

In 1964, the artist made his first foreign trip, to France, at the invitation of his wife's uncle and aunt. He stayed in Paris for three months, took creative thinking classes, and paid a visit to Pablo Picasso at his studio. That experience was crucial for Tsereteli, as it changed his understanding of what it was to be an artist. He was greatly impressed by Picasso's working methods: the virtuoso interplay of skill and imagination, and free shifting from painting and drawing to ceramics and bronze sculpture. During a later trip, he also became acquainted to Marc Chagall, taking inspiration from the child-like immediacy of his poetic dreamscapes in painting and stained glass.

After his return home, Tsereteli's career took a new turn when he became the chief designer of Soviet resort complexes on the Black Sea, notably in Pitsunda (1967) and Adler (1972). In these large-scale works, he got an opportunity to fulfill his ideas of combining monumental sculpture, architectural scenery, and vivid three-dimensional mosaic compositions with natural and symbolic motifs. These works were admired by David Alfaro Siqueiros, who flew from Mexico and visited the artist in 1972–1973. After the project in Pitsunda in 1967, Zurab Tsereteli was awarded the title of the Honored Artist of Georgia.

In the 1970s, the artist continued to carry out numerous important public projects in Tbilisi, Ulyanovsk, Yalta, and other cities. Each time, he strived to create a synthesis of media, including mosaics, stained glass, copper and bronze sculpture. Always looking for innovative ways to treat the material, he developed a unique method of crafting monumental cloisonné enamels, reconceiving this traditionally compact technique as a monumental art form. Significantly, in this period Tsereteli designed several Soviet embassies and consulates all around the world, including those in Brazil, Portugal, and Japan. While working in Brasilia and Rio de Janeiro, he became friends with the visionary architect Oscar Niemeyer.

In 1978–1979, Zurab Tsereteli was invited to the United States to teach painting as a visiting professor at the College at Brockport, State University of New York. His stay there was marked by two remarkable public sculptures that he donated to the College on behalf of the people of the USSR: *Prometheus* (*Light and Knowledge to the World*), installed in front of the Allen Administration Building, and *Joy and Happiness to All the Children of the World*, next to the Drake Memorial Library. One of the artist's most important works in the Western hemisphere, *Joy and Happiness to All the Children of the World* was created together with the Joseph P. Kennedy, Jr. Foundation in honor of the Special Olympics, which took place in Brockport in 1979. Zurab Tsereteli is an honorary professor of the College at Brockport.

Back in the USSR, Tsereteli was appointed the chief designer of the XXII Summer Olympic Games in Moscow (1980). That same year, he completed his ambitious copper relief frieze, *A Hymn to Man*, that crowns the Concert and Cinema hall of the Izmailovo Hotel Complex, constructed especially for the Olympics, and received the Order of the "Friendship of the Peoples." In 1981, the artist became a professor at the Tbilisi Academy of Arts, his alma mater.

In 1983, he created the large-scale *Friendship Forever* monument on Moscow's Tishinskaya Square (1983), dedicated to the historical bonds of good fellowship between Russia and Georgia. The architectural part of this monument was designed by the famous poet Andrey Voznesensky, a professional architect by training. In his hometown, Tsereteli initiated work on two important long-term projects: the monument to Saint Nina (1988–1994)—Georgia's holy patroness—and the *History of Georgia* complex (1985–present). The busy decade culminated in two prestigious international commissions. In 1988, the year the artist was elected an Academician of the USSR Academy of Arts, his sculptural composition *Break the Wall of Distrust* was installed in London on Cannon Street. Two years later, the *Good Defeats Evil* sculptural group, which reimagines the feat of Saint George slaying the dragon as an allegory of world peace in the modern age, was unveiled on the grounds of the United Nations Headquarters.

In the new post-Soviet Russia, Zurab Tsereteli continued to work on ambitious public commissions in Moscow, collaborating with big creative and technical teams. These projects were diverse in social functions and the artistic challenges they posed. He was the main designer of the War Memorial Complex on Poklonnaya Hill, the construction of which had been launched in the late 1980s and finished in 1995 to mark the 50th anniversary of the victory in World War II. He designed the "Okhotny Ryad" shopping and recreation center, with its promenade, on Manezhnaya Square next to the Kremlin (1993–1997). He was the chief artist in the rebuilding project of the Christ the Savior Cathedral (1994–1999), the most important house of worship of the Russian Orthodox Church. In 1996–1997, to commemorate the 300th anniversary of the Russian Navy, the artist created the 98-meter-tall monument to Peter the Great on the Moskva River. Also, in the same year, he contributed to the reconstruction of the Moscow Zoo.

In 1995, the 43.5-meter-tall sculptural monument titled *The Birth of the New Man* was inaugurated in Seville, Spain: it celebrated the European discovery of the New World by Christopher Columbus. The following year, another Andalusian city—Marbella—received the artist's public monument, titled *Victory*.

In 1997, Zurab Tsereteli was elected the President of the Russian Academy of Arts. Two years before, he established the Moscow Museum of Modern Art, which would officially open its doors in 1999 as the first state museum in the country entirely dedicated to modern and contemporary art. In autumn 1998, his first solo exhibition opened in Moscow at the New Manege and was dedicated to the memory of his beloved wife, Inessa. It was the start of numerous travelling shows of his works—paintings, drawings, bronzes, enamels—that followed in the 2000s–2010s in many cities in Russia, in Georgia, Latvia, Belarus, Kazakhstan, Kyrgyzstan, Bulgaria, Italy, France, the USA, Australia, China, and Japan.

In 2006, Zurab Tsereteli unveiled his 30-meter-tall sculptural monument *To the Struggle Against World Terrorism*, or *The Tear of Grief*, in Bayonne, New Jersey. It was donated to the United States as an official gift of Russia in the aftermath of the 9/11 attacks and in solidarity with the American people.

In 2007, the artist became the UNESCO Ambassador of Good Will. In 2009–2010, he was elected a Member of the European Academy of Sciences and Arts (Austria), honored with a title of Chevalier of the National Order of the Legion of Honor by the government of France, and a 1st Rank Order "For Services to Motherland" by the Russian government (in 2014, he became the Full Cavalier of this Order, having been previously awarded all of its ranks). In 2011, he received two awards from the Roman Academy of Fine Arts: the Prize "For Life in Art" and the International Giuseppe Sciacca Award for significant contribution to the arts. In 2014, the artist received the UNESCO Five Continents Medal for his contribution to world culture. A year later, he was elected a Member of the Chinese Academy of Fine Arts.

For Tsereteli, the period of 2000s–2010s has been very eventful in the sphere of public commissions. In 2005, his memorial *Holocaust* composition was donated by Russia to Israel and opened in Jerusalem. Among his sculptural monuments are those of writers Nikolai Gogol in Rome's Villa Borghese park (2002), Honoré de Balzac in Agde (2003), and Marina Tsvetaeva in St. Gilles Croix De Vie (2012). In the same year, the *Founding Fathers of the European Union* sculptural group was installed in Scy-Chazelles (Lorraine, France). Two years after, the monument to Pope John Paul II was placed next to the Notre-Dame de Paris cathedral facing the Seine.

In 2001, the Gallery of Arts of Zurab Tsereteli was opened in Moscow as part of the museum and exhibitions complex of the Russian Academy of Arts. He founded the Museum of Modern Art in Tbilisi (2012), which organizes regular exhibitions by Georgian and international artists. Zurab Tsereteli continues his active service as the President of the Russian Academy of Arts and the founding Director of the Moscow Museum of Modern Art. He works tirelessly, always experimenting as an artist, producing many new works in painting and graphic media, bronze and enamel, tapestry and stained glass, prints and ceramics, while channeling his energies into philanthropy, education, and public awareness of the visual arts.

James Hill is a leading British photographer and photojournalist. His images have won many of photography's most important prizes including World Press Photo, the Pulitzer Prize, the Visa d'Or at Perpignan's Visa Pour l'Image, and awards from The Overseas Press Club of America and the NPPA. Originally a news and war photographer, with many years spent in conflict zones in the former USSR, the Middle East, and Afghanistan, his work now is more feature- and project-based.
He has published four books and his work has been shown in solo exhibits in state and commercial galleries worldwide. His photographs are also in the permanent collections of the Pushkin Museum, the Moscow Museum of Multimedia/Moscow House of Photography, the Houston Museum of Fine Arts, as well as in institutional and private collections.

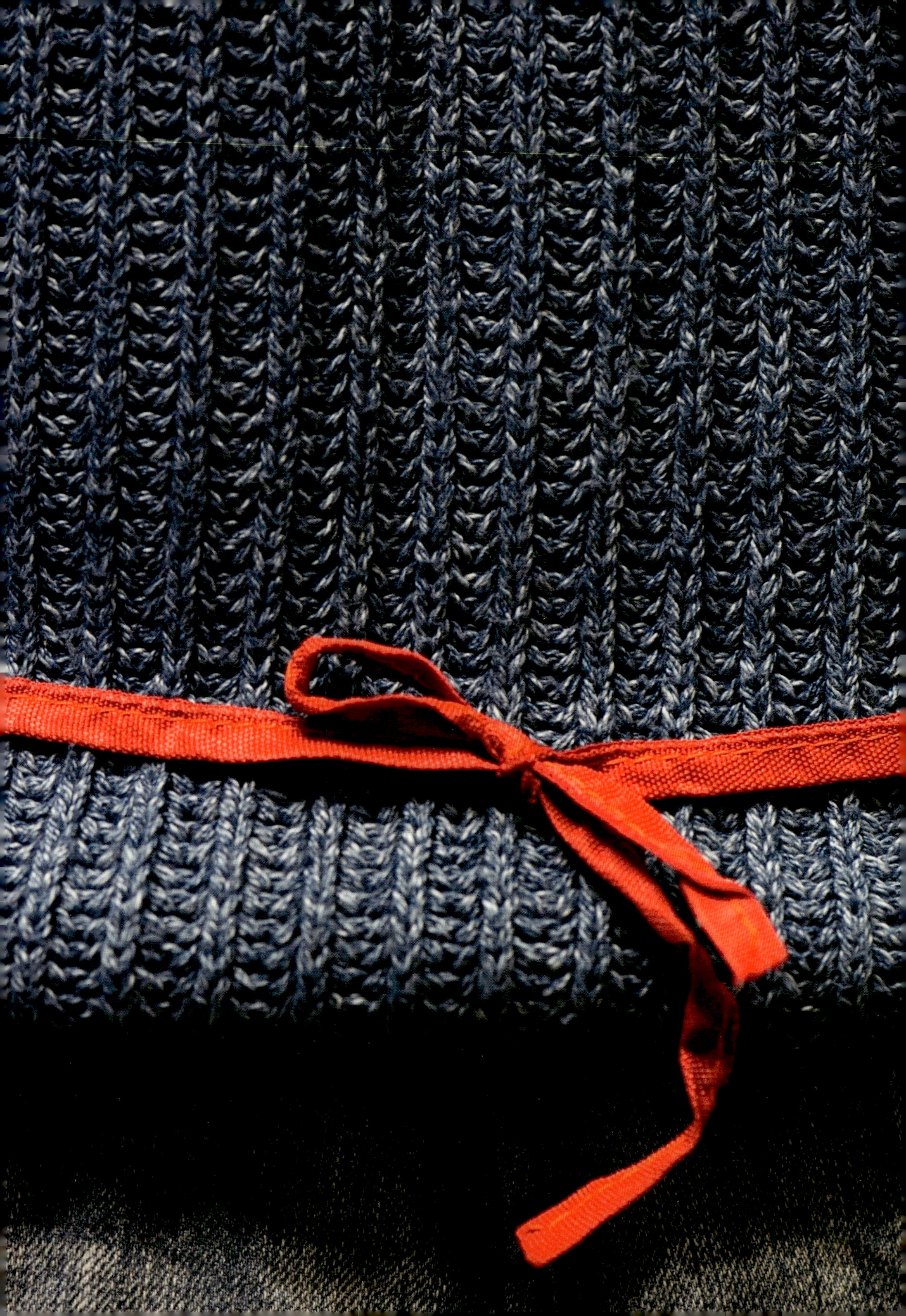

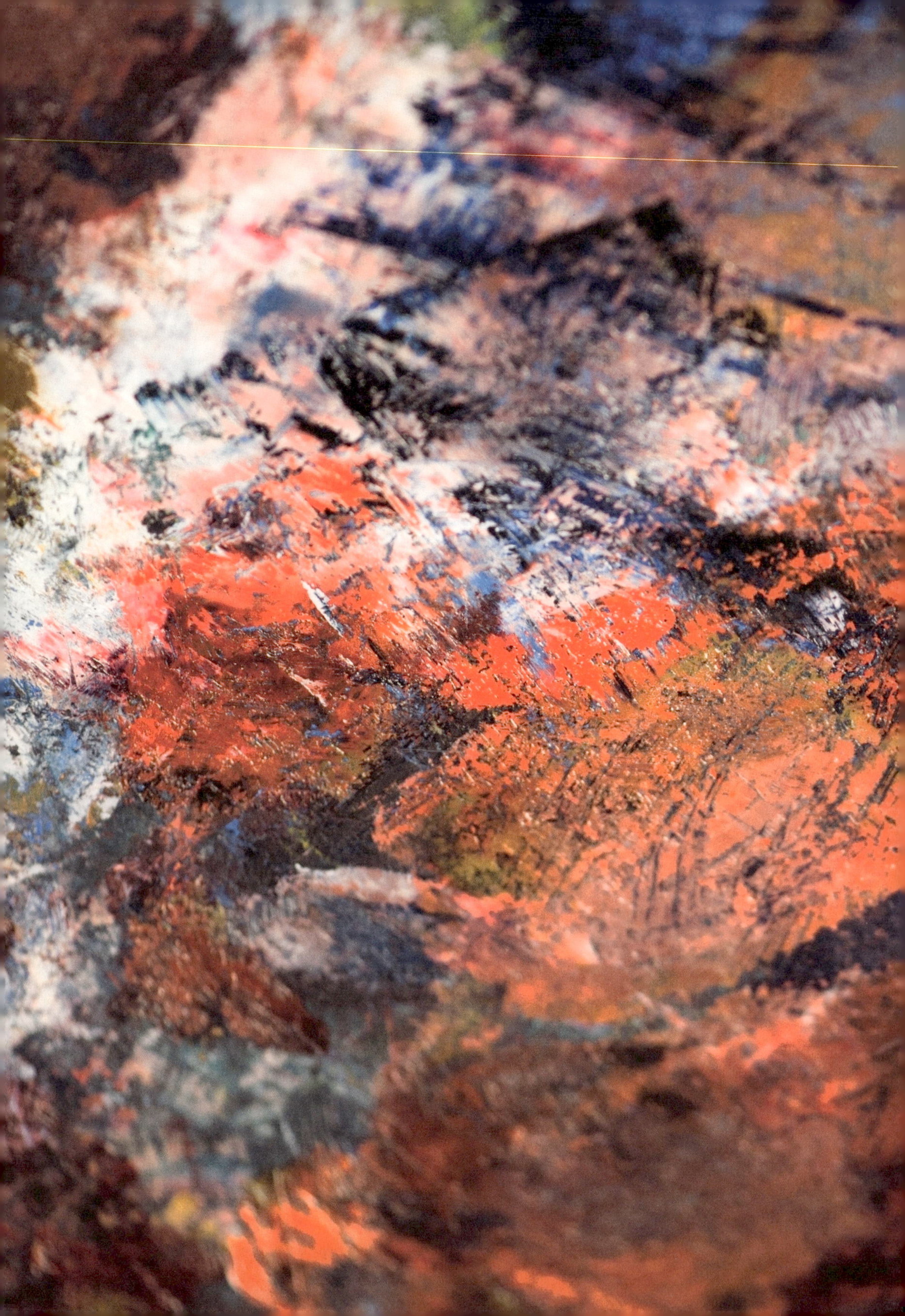